A History of the Oriental Club

Hugh Riches

with illustrations by Andrew McDowall

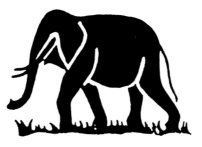

Published by the Oriental Club

Published in Great Britain by
Oriental Club

ISBN 0 9534594 0 3

Printed by Grillford Ltd, Milton Keynes

Contents

Acknowledgements

THIS BOOK was written on a computer which seeks to correct spelling errors and has insisted throughout the writing that Hanover Square should be Hangover Square. This insight was not available to my two predecessors as historians of the Oriental Club. Their work has provided much of the information in the following pages, and much pleasure. Alexander Baillie, the magnificent Baillie, published his History of the Oriental Club in 1901. He was clearly as much a participant in the history as its recorder, a high Victorian character who often shared dinner with his subjects. Denys Forrest published the first edition of his Oriental Club in 1968. It has been an invaluable source of material for the years before the club moved to Stratford House. Both are often quoted in the following work. I should also mention The Annuls of the Oriental Club, a fairly comprehensive list of all members before 1852, drawn up by Sir Henry Wheeler, who was chairman of the club in 1936.

This volume would have little beauty were it not for the wonderful artwork of Andrew McDowall.

I'm very grateful to the club secretary, who has provided every kindness a historian could desire, discovered treasured source materials and, above all, had tremendous patience. The club's committee has been likewise patient, as far as I know, ever since the late Berry Templeton commissioned a new history. Of course, all the staff at the Oriental have made the discovery of its past a delightful experience.

Several people have helped by reading parts of the manuscript and advising on content and style, some rather sternly, some with suspicious brevity, all with great generosity. I think almost every suggestion has been incorporated. My greatest thanks go to my family who have valiantly read and improved every draft as well as giving me unlimited support, generosity, kindness and understanding.

The mistakes, of course, are all mine.

Hugh Riches.
Stratford House,
September, 1998.

Chapter I

Foundation

IN THE book-lined splendour of the Royal Asiatic Society map room, on the 17th of February, 1824, a small group of middle-aged military gentlemen gathered to remember maharajas.

They were mostly senior field and flag officers of the Honourable East India Company, the army and the Royal Navy. They were battle hardened; many at Waterloo or the Nile, the majority in the innumerable conflicts and skirmishes fought to protect and preserve the British interests in the east. This tanned, polyglot group had travelled half the world, watched widows burn by the sacred Ganges, tasted a furnace of Indian spice, commanded thousands of armed men and parlayed with princes in golden throne rooms. Now they were home in cold, wet London, confined to English cooking and their gardens, reduced to conversations about cricket and the price of coal. They were bored.

Some of them had already ended their eastern careers. They had served in India under the governor-generalships of Warren Hastings and the Marquis Wellesley, bringing most of the sub-continent under British control. Others were the new men; younger, more expert in the science of government and perhaps a little less buccaneering. They had been Wellesley's proteges and, in turn, the proteges' proteges. These men were ambitious in the eastern administration but, due to misfortune or incompetence, they found themselves back in London.

Governor-general Wellesley had left India sixteen years before but his officers had continued his tradition of efficient, benevolent government. Chief among these were three men who did much to make the Indian empire respected in the east and acceptable back home. They were Charles Metcalf, Montstuart Elphinstone and John Malcolm. To these three must be added another; the soldier who had led Wellesley's forces in India, his little brother Arthur, now Duke of Wellington, who had also enjoyed some military success in Europe.

Wellington was not there at the Asiatic Society meeting but Elphinstone and Malcolm certainly were. They did not take a record but Malcolm's older brother Pulteney, an admiral who had served with Nelson, was probably present. These were the closest of the original members and the leading lights in the foundation of the Oriental Club. It is impossible to say who else joined them but they did agree to recruit some more likely friends and provide some succour for eastern officers and officials who found themselves becalmed and lonely in London. To this end they resolved to meet again at the same place a week later. Before that meeting a committee was to draw up a prospectus for a new club.

Dating the genesis of a body so intangible as a club is almost impossible, all the more so because the Oriental started so spontaneously and by small moments of evolution. Alexander Baillie reports only that the club was probably "conceived in the rooms of the Royal Asiatic Society." If that image is appropriate then it's story starts with a first kiss when, in some unrecorded, mythological conversation, Wellington suggested the idea to Malcolm. It continued with a conception when that small group gathered on the 17th of February. The gestation was brief. Birth was given on the 24th when Malcolm presided over a larger group at the Royal Asiatic Society which carried a resolution:

> That it appears to this meeting to be desirable to form a society on the plan set forth in the following prospectus, to be called the Oriental Club, to issue a prospectus and to nominate a committee.

It had clearly been a busy week. The original close group had obviously consulted with their old comrade Wellington and announced at the meeting that he was willing to accept the presidency of the club. A full and detailed prospectus had been drafted. It stated the purpose of the club:

> The British Empire in the East is now so extensive, and the persons connected with it so numerous, that the establishment of an institution where they may meet on a footing of social intercourse seems particularly desirable.

In addition to seeing old friends, members were to form "acquaintances and connections in their own country" and "keep up their knowledge of the actual state of our Eastern Empire." Those who have had the running of the club have rarely attempted to fulfil the prospectus' condition of creating a place to exchange information and study from the east. Malcolm and Wellington might have hoped for learned papers but lack of interest and the competition of the Asiatic Society soon destroyed any academic purpose for the club.

Nevertheless, there was to be a library and a reading room as well as a coffee room, regular house dinners and a concerted search for a building in which all this might be housed.

The speed with which the prospectus was drafted, in seven days between the 17th and 24th of February, shows in the occasional contradiction and compromise. Eligibility for membership was ambiguous. One clause states that the club should be for those;

> Having been resident or employed in the public service of His Majesty, or the East India Company, in any part of the East; belonging to the Royal Asiatic Society, being officially connected with the administration of our Eastern Governments abroad or at home.

Another clause is wider, welcoming members of the Bengal, Bombay, India and China Clubs as well as members of the Asiatic Society and clearly stating;

> That all persons who have resided or travelled or whose official situation connects them with that quarter of the globe, be considered eligible to become members.

The early nineteenth century legal meaning of 'persons' was similar to the modern sense except that it excluded those under 21 and all women.

The meeting agreed enviably generous membership fees: the entrance tariff was £15 and the annual subscription £6. These, it was decided, were far too generous and on St. Valentines Day, 1825, a general meeting increased the sums to £20 and £8 respectively.

John Malcolm had presided over both Royal Asiatic Society meetings and, after the second, walked away as the first chairman of the Oriental Club at the head of its first committee, a committee of forty-three men. As yet there were no other members.

THAT MEMBERSHIP would be recruited among a fairly specific category of men. It included some veterans but it was dominated by young middle-aged people, with the experience to find things wrong and the opportunity to put them right. They were Wellesley's trainees, the first generation to operate in the east with the ethos that Indians might benefit from British government, not just pay for the luxury of their governors. They were men of the eighteenth century living in the nineteenth. They were young in Georgian England at the peak of the Age of Enlightenment. Their generation was reactionary, understandably in the time of Bonaparte, but liberal in its reforms of empire and, within eight years, of democracy at home. The club was founded on a historical and cultural cusp. During the years after Waterloo power in England moved from a cheery squirarchy towards the brooding gloom of the dark Satanic mills.

Their fathers and grandfathers could have been described by Fielding or Byron, their sons and grandsons by Dickens or Kipling but the original members came somewhere in between. Whatever type of men made up the first membership, Jane Austen gave them no coverage.

So they were men at the end of a great epoch made by events, perhaps, like eager students of the Lambeth Walk in 1929, slightly surprised to find themselves retired colonels in 1949.

In the east, too, the original members worked their careers between two traditions. They had no particular objection to local customs, were willing to tolerate the ignition of the occasional widow and quite appreciative of the erotic shapes of Hindu temple walls and of Hindu women but they wanted to apply a form of comparatively just government alien to India. They had little of the evangelism and intentions of missionary improvement of their immediate successors and little of the rapacious corruption of their immediate predecessors. Theirs was the fair, tolerant generation before the missionaries, after the nabobs.

The nabobs, named as princes of India by those who could not pronounce 'nawab', had given those returning from the east a bad name. They were regarded as uncouth *arrivistes* who had more money than morals and, much worse, more money than manners. The officers of the East India Company who had made themselves rich by prize money, looting and corruption under Clive and Hastings were reviled in Britain. Indian vices were brought to Britain by people who aspired to the privileges of the aristocracy and had no trouble buying them (there were certainly, for example, some country house harems.) They were not quite from the land-owning class, they were brash and uncouth; in short, in the phrase of a late twentieth century nabob, they bought their own furniture.

Shockingly for the British establishment, that furniture often included a seat in the House of Commons. This might have been tolerable but the nabobs pushed up the price: they found it so infuriatingly easy to bribe voters or purchase their own rotten boroughs that the cost of Parliamentary seats suffered a bout of tremendous inflation during the late eighteenth century. In a House of 558 there were 26 nabob members between 1774 and 1780 and 45 between 1784 and 1790. Horace Walpole, the son of an earl, asked;

> What is England now? - A sink of Indian wealth, filled by nabobs... A senate sold and despised! A country overrun by horse-races! A gaming, robbing, wrangling, railing nation without principles, genius, character or allies.

Horace was clearly not fond of horses or gambling.

The new Indian power in politics was also feared because all the British, not just the snobs, knew of the violent opportunism that had made the nabob's fortunes. A pamphleteer complained of...

> Lacks and Crows [lakhs and crores] of rupees, sacks of diamonds, Indians tortured to disclose their treasure; cities, towns and villages ransacked and destroyed, jaghires [tax districts] and provinces purloined; nabobs dethroned, and murdered, have found the delights and constituted the religions of the Directors [of the Company] and their servants.

By the turn of the nineteenth century those returning from the east were unwelcome in polite society and unloved by the impolite mass. Twenty-four years later the prejudice was weaker but still overpowering despite the hero Wellington's declaration that he had learned all he knew about soldiering in India.

For all the support the original members enjoyed from that field marshal and the fraternal love of an admiral of the Royal Navy, many of them suffered a second prejudice. They were Company officers not king's officers. Even Wellington, whose words became true by his speaking them, could not eradicate the snobbery and envy that oppressed his friends. Officers in the King's army were paid little. Their parents bought their commissions at great expense and every promotion afterwards until they had a regiment. It was the luxury of inherited wealth that made a man a gentleman in the royal service, and he served for little but the glory of it, although the lucky ones could find loot like any other soldier. Officers of the Company army in India were promoted by merit and, whatever their patriotism and love for the mad king and his regent, they were honest enough to fight only in the hope of a fortune. The distinction was fairly simple: the King's men were gentlemen and the Company's were players.

When a King's officer returned from the east he kept his rank and his status. When a Company officer returned he lost his rank precisely as his ship came west of the Cape. Glorious but poor, King's men strutted happily around St James with much gilt on their epaulettes hating the Company men who met them in silky civilian clothes and a fortune from Calcutta at Couttes. The first chairman of the Oriental Club, Sir John Malcolm, a Company man, was everywhere a belted knight but he was a colonel and then major-general only east of Istanbul. The prejudice was limited to the two armies: a high proportion of king's officers on the original committee of the Oriental were commissioned in the Royal Navy, a service which never tolerated a grudge.

The men attracted to the Oriental Club might have had one more characteristic in common which separated them from the society they re-entered back in London. They had watched dhows sail the warm waters of Bombay and Brahmins walk on burning coals, they had ridden elephants to hunt tigers and enjoyed the hospitality of the world's most expert seraglios. The gossip of fashionable salons and gaming tables and the latest dance in St. James were unlikely to excite such an exotic group. Those who had seen the Taj Mahal were not so easily impressed by a society headed by a foppish king with a fantasy pavilion in Brighton. The original membership was a companionship slightly apart from its contemporaries.

By 1824 the resentment against the Company had been weakened by the reforms of Wellesley and Malcolm in India and a social and political unity forged by the common fight against Napoleon. The 'Indians', as those returning from the east were known, were not actually excluded from other clubs. When the United Service Club, 'The Senior', was founded in 1815 it specified that "general and field officers of the East India Company's service," should be welcome, and that they must be represented on the committee. Malcolm himself was one of the Senior's first committee members, along with three other Company officers. Nevertheless, a certain *froidure* was evident. When the Junior United Service Club was founded, three years after the Oriental, it is said that Company officers were systematically blackballed.

The unhappy legacy of the nabobs and the snobbery of king's officers ensured that the Indians could never count on a warm welcome. No doubt this was at least one reason why, when they met at the Royal Asiatic Society, it appeared "to this meeting to be desirable to form a society..."

ON THE evening of the 24th of February, 1824, the Oriental Club was a few hours old with a committee of 43 and a membership of 43. This slightly unbalanced ratio was to be corrected by a recruitment campaign of such Byzantine complication that some original members would be unrecognised and ejected at the door while others were billed for their subscriptions for years before ever they had heard of the place. The process was not simplified by the committee's decision to elect up to 400 members without ballot and send the prospectus to chosen officers of the Company, only sometimes with an invitation to join. Mr James Erskine was denied access to the club in 1842, furiously claiming that Monstuart Elphinstone had proposed him four years previously and that Malcolm himself had told him that all senior officers were entitled to automatic membership. Erskine did not take his rebuff graciously, telling all his Indian friends of "the mode in which affairs are conducted at the club…", and was never elected.

Ten days less than a year passed before the entrance fee and the subscriptions were increased from the estimate of that first full meeting. They were not to rise again until 1882. Those who became members on the first tariff are those that earlier historians call the "Original Members", covered with all the glory that those capitals bestow.

The original terms were available to all gentlemen living out east for eighteen months from February 1824 who were not required to pay the subscription until they returned and started to use the club. Months passed as ships brought them the news that they were eligible for a new London club. Months passed as their applications returned. Further months passed as the news of the success or failure of their election, on papers now very salty, came back out to India. The consequent chaos was inescapable.

Captain Roe thought himself elected and foresaw a fine welcome when he came to London in 1830 only to discover that his application had been rejected in 1825. A quarter of a century after the club's foundation Mr Bannerman of the Madras Civil Service walked confidently through the doors of the Oriental Club to be rebuffed, his application for membership having been withdrawn by his London agents in 1837. In 1859 poor Sir Charles Gray, who had joined in London at the foundation, came back for the first time, having seen war and mutiny, to find that his membership had ceased in 1841.

Equally, complete strangers were to be astonished by their membership. When Mr Monckton was asked to pay his subscription he refused because, "subsequent to becoming a member he discovered that he never intended to join, but had done so under the belief that it was the same as the East India Service Club." The committee chose not to return Mr Monckton's entrance fee. A future governor of Ceylon, one of many Sir Colin Campbells, was adamant that he was never a member when asked for his fee. One man, entertained at the club by a friend in the strangers' room was utterly delighted to find, all unknowingly, that he had been a member for years. Lieutenant-Colonel James Alexander was elected in 1829, left for the Bengal Horse Artillery in 1831, and returned 23 years later to find himself unrecognised at the door. The name of this hero of the Afghan and Sikh wars had simply been forgotten on the membership list during his absence.

When the committee met on the 5th of September, 1859, it finally learnt the identity of a long standing member, Mr John Power Eyre, of the Bengal Civil Service. Nobody seemed to be able to put a face to the name. His proposer, Mr Boyd, finally confessed to having put up John Power and, in all good courtesy, followed his name with the appellation 'Esq.', which, in his hand-writing, had looked like the second

Sir John Malcolm, founder of the Oriental Club.

barrel of a surname. The Oriental did not discriminate between members on merely existential grounds.

The first large gathering of members, most of whom were certain of their membership, was held on the 7th of June, 1824. The first committee had the 300 members they needed to make the club viable in March and by this first general meeting the club numbered 540. The founders had hoped that the membership would not exceed 600; by June, 1825, it was 744. Within months of Malcolm summoning a group of friends to the Royal Asiatic Society it was clear that there was need for an Oriental Club.

THAT ORIGINAL gathering had more in common than their eastern service and the influence of the Marquis Wellesley. If not all close friends, they were all known to and admired by John Malcolm.

This soldier, scholar and administrator was born in 1769, the fourth son among eight boys and seven girls in the family of a humble but fertile tenant farmer near Langholme in Eskdale, Dumfriesshire. Of those sons, four were to die knights, two of them admirals, one a commander of marines and John a major-general.

After twelve years running wild across the country, and almost utterly uneducated, he made a suitably dashing impression at the Company head-quarters and took his commission as an ensign. His ship sailed for Madras a year later.

There he found a corrupt administration and an army depressed after unhelpful wars against Hyda Ali, the dashing usurper of the throne of Mysore. Malcolm thrived. One contemporary described him as "quite illiterate" but literacy was not an important aspect of life in the Madras presidency. The teenage officer soon grew to enjoy all the delights of the British in India during the late eighteenth century. He became an excellent rider, huntsman and, particularly, a brilliant shot. Unfortunately, but almost inevitably, he was a useless gambler, playing very high and amassing very large debts. He was known as the "Boy Malcolm", famous for "overflowing spirits that made him riotous."

By the time he was nineteen he wrote to his parents telling them that he was a "reformed character", a phrase usually more accurate from the pen of a magistrate than of any man describing himself. Nevertheless, Malcolm had developed some serious and useful interests. He was no longer "quite illiterate" but now a keen student, devouring history and local languages. Most importantly, he learned Persian, the language of diplomacy in India and of the civilisation on which he would be expert.

He got his first break during the 1792 campaign against Tippu Sultan, Hyda Ali's son. Lord Cornwallis defeated the Sultan, took his sons hostage, as the club's Mather Brown painting records, and hoped that an obscure sepoy regiment, the 29th Native Infantry, would not get in the way of his more prominent units. The 29th did have the useful 23 year old Lieutenant Malcolm whose language skills were noticed and exploited by Cornwallis. The young officer was made official interpreter to Sir John Kennaway, chief negotiator of the treaty that humbled Tippu. The Mather Brown includes Malcolm, depicting him as a colonel. He did not quite hold such rank but he had been noticed by the big men in India. By the time he was in his early twenties Malcolm had had official dealings with both Cornwallis, the man who had been defeated by the treacherous rebels of the thirteen colonies in America, and with Tippu, the Tiger of Mysore.

After a year back home Malcolm was ordered east again. Alured Clerke commanded a force that had already taken Cape Town before it arrived in India. Malcolm's great mentor would be commander-in-chief of Madras, of India and a field marshal. He would also be one of those who met Malcolm at the Royal Asiatic Society in February, 1824, and served on the first committee.

Alured Clerke had never expected his military career to succeed east of Aden. In his youth he had the strange misfortune to be "that handsome young captain", desirable enough to have had one of the king's daughters fall in love with him. George III would have none of such romantic nonsense and made sure that the delightful officer was posted to the other side of the world. Clerke never lost his charms: in the early 1830s, well into his eighties, the field marshal dined with a much younger woman, no older than 75. When Clerke rose to say good night she complained "Were you not going away after having only kissed my hand?" The old soldier was as gallant as ever she hoped.

Clerke was one of those who provided Malcolm with his education, not that he needed teaching in politics or the literature of several languages. Clerke showed his protege that the British in India need not be nabobs: Malcolm wrote that;

> He is a declared foe to all dark dealings, and to peculation, and in everything that regards the Government, he is scrupulously just ...He never will himself make an indirect half-penny, nor allow any person he can control to do it.

Malcolm admired this new attitude. He was no puritan, continued to enjoy the drink, the gaming table, the hunt and the women, but he was honest enough not to expect a venal fortune or hope that the people of India might suffer a government of corruption. He might have remembered his grandfather, a minister in that stern Church of Scotland. Having been their student, it is more likely that he was one of the first of the British to learn to respect Indians.

He was soon joined in the sub-continent by men of like mind. The Wellesley boys arrived in 1798, the Marquis as governor-general and his younger brother, Arthur, later Duke of Wellington, in command of a battalion. The Marquis, then Lord Mornington, stopped off in Madras on the way to his appointment in Calcutta. He received papers by the young Malcolm on the local situation and the danger still presented by Tippu and the French. The new governor-general wrote to the new governor of Madras, Lord Clive, son of the victor of Plassey, that;

> Captain Malcolm is an officer of great worth, of extremely good sense, and well acquainted with the country languages, remarkably diligent, active and zealous.

He passed two of Malcolm's reports to Henry Dundas, chairman of the Company's board of control, a cabinet post, adding that "Captain Malcolm is a very promising young man. I have appointed him assistant to the resident of Hyderabad."

Poor John Malcolm was nothing but a promising bureaucrat before he met the talented colonel of the 33rd Foot, the governor-general's younger brother Arthur. This officer shared Malcolm's concerns in public life and his delights in private life. The future duke and his officers knew how to throw a party, according to one chronicler: "Indeed, a more severe debauch I never was engaged in, in any part of the world."

As the governor-general's agent, Malcolm was attached to Arthur's column in the second Battle of Serangapatam, in which Tippu died with his back to the palace, and which gave the Company the rule of Mysore. A commission was set up to establish government, headed by Arthur and with Malcolm as first secretary. The partnership was soon divided by orders that Malcolm, the brilliant linguist, should head an embassy to the court of the Shah of Persia.

The 'king of kings', successor of Cyrus and Darius and Xerxes, had never received a British embassy before 1801. He was delighted with this first ambassador. The 30-year old Captain Malcolm intended to persuade the shah to intervene against the Amir of Afghanistan, who threatened the northern plains of India. Malcolm and the shah became close; the Company officer impressed by the hospitality of the emperor, the emperor intrigued to hear Persian spoken in a soft Lowland accent.

Malcolm was to lead two more missions to the Persian court, in 1807 and 1810. When he last departed the shah cried: "Farewell, Malcolm, my friend," a remarkable compliment in the imperial etiquette.

Until 1805 Malcolm acted as the special agent and private secretary to the governor-general, who now inherited the marquisate and the name Wellesley. Wherever there might be trouble the British demanded that the marquis "Send Malcolm." The biggest trouble was in the Deccan where he was always in close touch with Arthur during the Assaye, Argaum and Gawilghur campaigns. Their friendship was sealed.

The career of the marquis declined on his recall, largely due to his libido. His brother, when duke, wrote:

> I wish that Wellesley was castrated ...it is lamentable to see talent and character and advantages, such as he has thrown away on whoring.

Malcolm and Arthur spent the last two months before the Wellesleys' recall together in Mysore. As he sailed from Madras, Arthur wrote "I hope you will take care to keep me informed in England of all kinds of events ...and so God bless you." They often corresponded. Malcolm kept his old comrade in touch with a girl-friend in Madras (Arthur could be a little hypocritical about his brother's amours) and the victor of the Peninsular sent accounts of Salamanca and Vitoria almost before the slaughter ended.

After ten years they met again in Paris, where Wellington (who had finally settled on a name and kept it) had invited Malcolm to help him celebrate the defeat of Bonaparte. The duchess was a tiresome woman and the duke was clearly glad of the company of another soldier who no longer sought his patronage. No doubt Malcolm, like all the general staff in Paris, enjoyed the small sexual irony of the duke's love life: Wellington's lover was Giuseppina Grassini, a woman of diplomatic pillow talk. She had previously been one of the seven mistresses of the Emperor Napoleon. Duke Arthur's wars became personal.

Of course, Wellington would have further work near Brussels in the summer of 1815. Malcolm returned to India to command in a further Maratha war, leading the charge into battle and, at six foot and six inches, terrifying his foes. Triumphant, he first governed the central state of Malwa, delivering its subjects from slavery, and then, having established the Oriental Club during an unwelcome hiatus at home, he rose to the governorship of Bombay from 1827 to 1830.

Malcolm came home in 1831 a major-general in the Company service, an ambassador, statesman, governor and knight grand cross of the Bath. He was 61, his sons were in India, his friends were at the Oriental Club. He had not quite achieved the pinnacle, the governor-generalship, but he never had the background or patronage required for that eminence. His career was over and he needed a hobby, so he entered the House of Commons. It was not a glorious moment: his instincts were always liberal and democratic but he opposed the Great Reform Bill simply out of loyalty to the chief of its Parliamentary resistance. The Duke of Wellington was fighting Reform in the House of Lords.

"Quite illiterate", he was, when he went to Madras in 1783. His literary achievements were to include the first English *History of Persia,* two volumes of a *Political History of India,* another two volumes of *A Memoir of Central India* and various other memoirs and sketches. The Persian work is still crucial to scholars of that land. His three volume *Life of Robert, Lord Clive* was not quite complete when he died in 1833.

He had made a two hour speech in the Company's Court of Proprietors when its Charter was up for renewal under the India Act. He pleaded passionately the case for the Company's achievements and, as his points were finished, he fainted, the victim of a stroke. For ten days he was cheered by the visits of Wellington, but then John Malcolm died.

Six years before, in 1827, when Malcolm was about to sail to the governorship of Bombay his friends organised a farewell dinner. The Duke of Wellington, first and only president of the Oriental Club, stood up to speak of its first chairman and founder. He said;

It is now 30 years since I formed an intimate friendship with Sir John Malcolm. During that eventful period there has been no operation of consequence, no diplomatic measure, in which my friend has not borne a conspicuous part. Alike distinguished by courage and talent, the history of his life, during that period, would be the history of the glory of his country in India.

MALCOLM HAD given the club an identity, a constitution, a committee and a large membership by the summer of 1824. The members just needed somewhere to go.

The Oriental Club's first home was in Grosvenor Street, only a few hundred metres south of Stratford Place towards Berkeley Square. Negotiations were started on the 7th of April, 1824 to hire the upper part of number 16, the premises of Seddons upholsterers. A deal was made and reported to the general meeting of the 7th of June. Seddons insisted that their entrance be separate from that of the club, and such separation required the construction of a new front door, a duplicate just next to the original, and a new staircase. With admirable and enviable efficiency, the builders were out by July. The club leased its first rooms, in the heart of Mayfair, at the rate of £1,200 for a year, or £2,300 for two.

It would remain an upstairs lodger for four years. Wise Wellington was thinking more of the coldness found by Indian officers in other clubs than the fantastic history of London property values when he gave his famous, probably apocryphal advice to Malcolm: "Have your own club. Own your own property." The first chairman was determined to heed such a sensible sentiment. Until 1828 the committee was dedicated to buying a club-house. As it turned out, the club bought a house, knocked it down and built a strange, dark, squat palazzo.

Members were in a slightly awkward position with regard to the late Georgian equivalents of estate agents, who were often architects touting for work. Malcolm had given the business to two of them, each ignorant of the other, each assuming themselves beloved of the club. They were George Basevi and Benjamin Wyatt. Basevi was a distinguished man, student of the great Sir John Soane, who built the Bank of England and whose house and collection in Lincoln's Inn Field became a treasure of London. Basevi was architect of the Fitzwilliam museum in Cambridge and, in 1845, mortal victim of a fall from the stately top of Ely Cathedral, which he was surveying in the company of the young Gilbert Scott. It had been Basevi, quite a famous architect, who found Grosvenor Street for the club.

His rival, Wyatt, was always going to get the big job. He was the insider, well known to the Wellesleys and thus to Malcolm. Wyatt had left Oxford broke from gambling and gone to India as a writer, a junior Company clerk, in 1798. He entered the governor-general's circle and became a friend of the Marquis Wellesley. He did not much like the east - found it rather hot - and returned to Britain in 1802. Three years later the Wellesleys were recalled and Arthur, always one to look after old friends, gave him a job as his private secretary when he took the office of Chief Secretary in Ireland.

The Wellesleys were an Irish family but they didn't like to admit it. When Duke Arthur once was reminded of his nationality he told the impertinent questioner that "being born in a stable does not make one a horse."

Nevertheless, the Irish appointment made Wyatt one of the magic group. In December, 1824, Malcolm sacked Basevi and sent him £50 for his "zeal and activity." Basevi, by far the best man for the job, was rightly proud. He returned the money with a note that he had been;

> ...actuated by an ambition not unnatural to obtain the distinction of being appointed architect to the club (which honour I had been given to understand could only be obtained by such services) and not by motives of pecuniary emolument, but if I had thought of such acknowledgement I should not have considered the services and the expenses involved (little as I am disposed to value the former) to be at all remunerated by the note sent me.

He was terribly cross; only angry architects use words like 'actuated' and 'emolument'.

The committee swallowed the rebuff, banked the cash and gave Wyatt the job.

Various locations were scouted: the Marquis of Anglesey's house on Burlington Street; the Duke of Portland's house on St James's Square; other plots in King Street and Bruton Street. If all the members by the summer of 1824 had paid their entrance fees and their first year's subscriptions the club would have held £15,540. A property in St James's Square was offered for £28,000, a plot on St James's Street was available only for rent for £1,800 per year. Under the Duke's good advice, the traditional precincts of clubland were clearly unobtainable.

This was not necessarily unwelcome to the older members. A tradition had grown up during the early years of the nineteenth century that those retiring from eastern service tended to live around Harley Street, Cavandish and Hanover Squares; the 'Indians' were hiving just around Oxford Street. Consequently, the Oriental Club,

Number 18, Hanover Square in the
late nineteenth century.

The perilous staircase at number 18.

Hanover Square's spacious drawing room.

with its complement of refugees from Bengal and Punjab, would find its address named for a city in Saxony.

On the 2nd of March, 1826, the committee, chaired by Malcolm, decided to offer £14,000 for the freehold, the fee simple absolute in possession, of number 18, Hanover Square, and to throw in another couple of hundred pounds for the furniture. Negotiation commenced.

A Mr Trant did the negotiating and achieved a great victory over the furniture but allowed the freehold price to rise from an offer of £14,000 to an agreement of £14,300. Wyatt, the well-connected but mediocre architect, desperately wanted the chance to practice some architecture. He had his way: the building present on the site would be knocked down and another £14,000 spent on a new construction. After all the hard bargaining by Mr Trant, Wyatt decided that another £4,000 were required for new furniture. He worked on commission.

He insisted that recovered material from the demolished house would return £3,000. His accuracy was typical of his builder's trade; the recovered materials returned the sum of £1,028, 12s, 6d.

The Oriental Club had lived for three years before it was in deep debt. A permanent home, owned outright, would cost the members almost £33,000, a little more than twice as much money as the club possessed.

"Send for Malcolm;" he had foreseen financial trouble. Three years before he had persuaded 100 members to invest £160 each on the security of "any house which the club could satisfactorily buy." The list of the original hundred signatures is framed and displayed in the club, and includes the names of future governors-general, directors and one future prime minister, Wellington. These autographs doubled the capital of the club.

At least they would when all the subscribers were chastised into paying up. On the 29th of May, 1828, the reluctant ones received a letter stating that;

I am directed by the Committee of Management once more to call upon you for your subscription of £160 for providing a new Club House, and to observe that the means hitherto taken to procure a suitable House for the Club were adopted on the faith of gentlemens' punctuality [in] meeting the engagements into which they had voluntarily entered; and the Committee do not feel themselves authorised to proceed while any doubt exists as to the payments being made good. I am further to request that you will pay the sum of £160 on or before the 10th of June.

Work started immediately.

NUMBER EIGHTEEN Hanover Square had been purchased from Josias du Pre Alexander, an original member of the club, member of Parliament for the rotten borough of Old Sarum, director of the Company and proud father of five exceptionally beautiful daughters. His own father was the first Earl of Caledon and one of the greatest, or worst of nabobs. Josias, on selling number 18, moved his home a couple of doors away to number 16, Hanover Square.

With such a background and such a career, Josias Alexander knew precisely how lascivious and lecherous the members of the Oriental Club would be. He also knew that his five fine daughters were now living within a fall of breeches from the new club house and he would not take risks. The committee received a letter demanding that the new building have its front door on the Tenterden Street elevation rather than on the square, as it had been, so that members could not disport themselves on the steps and leer across at the pulchritude opposite. In fact, it would have taken peepers with periscopes to see much of the Alexander maidens. Nevertheless, Josias was a powerful man and an original member. Saving any pride the committee might have lost by seeming too obedient, Wyatt conveniently insisted that the entrance must be on Tenterden Street for reasons of pure architectural aesthetics.

Wyatt's building was no Parthenon or, more appropriately, no Taj. It was so similar to the house he built for Crockfords at the top of St James's Street (later the Devonshire) that the critic Sir John Summerson described the two together in his great *Georgian London*. He wrote:

> Both were ponderous in scale (like his earlier Drury Lane Theatre) with great slabs of Corinthian pilastar surmounted by an entablature of coarse Greek profile... The Oriental has a poor site, facing north ...Here Wyatt pilastered the ends and slightly recessed the centre (again like Drury Lane). The Oriental is a dull building, rendered ugly now by towering increments on its skyline.

Summerson was not a tolerant man: he went on to describe Crockfords, one of Wellington's favourite haunts, as "a gambling hell of the most lavish and patrician character."

Inside, however, the new Oriental Club would have almost all its members could desire. On two stories, it had a large coffee room 60 feet along the square with a matching drawing room above. Over a billiard room and a dining room Wyatt placed the secretary's office and the crucial card room, cause of much future grief. All were reached through a sombrely impressive hall and the compulsory grand staircase. Forty-seven steps, on two flights were required to elevate the members to the height of the stately downstairs ceilings. Surviving photographs show this to be a dark, cavernous, perilous ascent.

With all the logic of late Georgian architecture, the kitchens occupied a sub-basement in which the waiters would start their long, cooling hike to the dining and coffee rooms.

Perhaps the exterior of 18, Hanover Square was not the most inspired facade in London and perhaps Wyatt had, " great competance but small invention," but his other work might give him a little more credit than his critics suggest. He designed the Duke of York's column in Waterloo Place and, blessed by the ever patient patronage of Wellington, the face of Apsley House. These, and the Drury Lane Theatre, are much more than jobbing architecture, and the members of the Oriental Club soon found Wyatt's creation a comfortable and convenient home.

In function, if not form, the club had commissioned, and paid £33,000 for a tailor-made house which proved a perfect fit.

THE FABRIC of the club was complete by the end of the 1820s. A building was ready in Hanover Square, the finances were deeply in the red but under control and the membership list was healthy even if it was to remain a little confused for 30 years or more. The Oriental had become a thriving and complicated business operating for the benefit of members who did not wish to be burdened with administration. Malcolm, as ever, had found a solution.

In April, 1824, within weeks of the foundation, Malcolm had appointed the club's first secretary, Thomas Cornish, who was paid a mere £200 per year for which he would "give up the whole of his time to the service of the club, and not to hold any other situation." Cornish's spidery hand would record the progress of the club for almost two decades during which nobody had anything but the greatest trust in a loyal servant.

The secretary handled a gentle succession of power in 1828, as the club eased itself into its new home. John Malcolm's career had finally found its former impetus and he was preparing for his governorship of Bombay. He handed over the chair to one of the club's many sailors, natural friends and protectors of the Company and its trade on the waves. Vice-Admiral Sir Richard King, baronet and second chairman of the club, had been at sea since he was 14 years old and became commander-in-chief of the East Indies station in 1816. He was a worthy successor to one who had served under Wellington. Twenty-three years before he took the chair of the Oriental Club King had sat on a gun in the great cabin of Victory with his brother captains as they received Nelson's final fighting orders off Cape Trafalgar.

Of the first inhabitants of Hanover Square, many were old friends of Wellington and Malcolm, the Wellesley connections who shared the humane and respectful vision of Indian government that dominated the early nineteenth century. Many were sailors, veterans of eastern waters and friends of Malcolm's two admiral brothers. Unsurprisingly, there were an awful lot of Scots.

The only real common denominator was their shared experience of the east. They were sociable but they had seen things unimaginable in other clubs so they were also exotically exclusive; a companionship slightly separate from the London life around them. They had inherited a tradition of war-like looting and they had bequeathed the British Empire.

Chapter II

Orient

IN WATERS four degrees, 25 minutes south, 129 degrees, 30 minutes east, the floor of the Banda Sea rises to form an island two miles long by half a mile wide. A walk around it takes no more than an hour. It has only ever had a sparse population, no buildings that survive much more than the warm breeze, and no source of fresh water.

It is Pulo Run, the first possession of the British Empire in the East.

When the British took the island, in 1603, their experience of sailing further than the capes was largely confined to government sponsored piracy. Drake had made his global raids on Spanish gold and shipping 23 years before, returning with a hold full of valuable cloves taken from Ternate. The sea dogs had resisted the Great Armada in 1588, and several more just as dangerous, and John Hawkins and his successors had founded a lucrative slave trade on the triangle from Bristol to the west African coast to the West Indies, but few British sailors, corsair or commercial, had ventured around Good Hope or Cape Horn.

So they were brave men, mariners and merchants, who celebrated the last night of the sixteenth century with the news that their consortium, led by Sir Thomas Smythe, had received a royal charter from Queen Elizabeth to form the 'The Company of Merchants of London trading into the East Indies'. Their structure and composition were to change often over the next two and a half centuries, as was their name. Eventually the institution they founded for the financing of a single voyage was to be known as the Honourable East India Company, administering India and making some men rich enough to want a club in London. Before such glory merchants needed something to buy and sell. The markets for stolen Spanish gold and stolen African labour were pretty much wrapped up by the crown and Bristol, and later Liverpool, traders. The eastern trade had the most precious treasure and, perhaps, the oldest cargo. 'Johnny' Company was formed to trade in spice.

Eastern spice had excited the palates of the Caesars and been traded through the Middle East and the Indus valley for centuries before the fall of Rome. Ancient texts contain some mention of frankincense and myrrh. They were rare and thus valuable, although the Arab suppliers were never above exaggerating their rarity. Cassia grew in shallow lakes guarded by winged animals, they said, and cinnamon grew in deep yellow valleys infested with venomous serpents. Pliny the Elder recognised marketing when he wrote that;

> ...all these tales, however, have been evidently invented for the purpose of enhancing the price of these commodities.

The European demand continued throughout the middle ages, providing one sound economic reason for the occasional crusade to capture the Holy Land with its roads to the Indian Ocean ports. Frankish domains in Acre, Antioch and Jerusalem were the first achievements of European imperialism since the fall of Rome. The destruction of a Venetian monopoly in the spice trade was the pious spur that sent many princes to take the cross. They failed. The cunning, half-blind, old Doge Enrico Dandolo offered the impoverished knights of the Fourth Crusade ample hospitality on the Lido. The only problem was that he refused to lend them any boats to get off the island until they promised to sack Constantinople, his chief competitor in the Eastern Mediterranean. His hijack of this mission of Christ ensured that Venice eliminated her spice rival. The Bride of the Sea retains her Byzantine spoils: the emperor's bronze horses still gallop in the sky above the Piazza San Marco.

The treacherous doge was buried in the city he had destroyed. When, in 1220, the newly powerful emperor Michael XVIII retook Constantinople, Dandolo's body was exhumed and thrown into the streets where "...even the dogs would not chew on his bones."

As the reformation and the renaissance began to galvanise Europe the stars lost their mystery, the compass was understood in the maritime nations and men dared to sail out of sight of land. In fourteen-hundred and ninety-two Columbus sailed the ocean in completely the wrong direction. His objective, however, was the same as that of his more successful Portuguese rivals: he wanted to break the Venetian, and increasingly Genoan, stranglehold on the trade in eastern spice.

That herbal treasure had always reached Arabs and Venetians by way of India. The sub-continent grew its own spices, as valued as any other, but it was also the global distribution point of more exotic wares from South East Asia and, especially, the islands of the Indonesian archipelago. Ceylon was a particularly busy point of exchange when the Europeans first came into the Indian Ocean. The Portuguese won the race to India, sailing home the first Western caravels to carry oriental spices in 1501. Eighteen years later a Spanish ship, laden with cloves, returned directly from the Spice Islands, the sole survivor of the first circumnavigation and in mourning for her dead master, Ferdinand Magellan. The ship's name was prophetic of the future of European imperialism in the East. She was called *Victoria*.

These avaricious seamen circled a flat planet, pushed the horizon out of sight of land and bound together antipodal civilisations. 'The Great Voyages of Discovery' are remembered by the descendants of the discoverers; 'The Great Arrivals of Thieving Brutal Christians' are as accurately remembered by the descendants of the discovered.

The Iberian adventurers were not helped by the domestic, dynastic politics of fifteenth century Spain and Portugal. Innumerable and fertile infantas flew from one court to the next, the nations were united and torn apart and government was done by a cruel mixture of prayer book and steel. Moreover, attractive as the spice trade was, South American gold did tend to concentrate the mind: a grandee's dinner was all the more grand for the gleaming plate beneath rather than for the pepper sprinkled from above. Before the turn of the sixteenth century the East Indies were no longer dominated by the Iberians but by a new nation, freshly liberated from Spanish Hapsburg, Catholic occupation. When the British arrived on Pulo Run they found themselves in the predominantly Dutch East Indies.

James Lancaster commanded a small fleet that would have been happy to sail against lakes guarded by winged animals and yellow valleys of vipers if that meant they could find the peculiar botany of Pulo Run. The island was largely covered by *myristica fragrans*, the fruit of which bore a husky membrane, mace, and a sweet kernel, nutmeg. In the Banda Sea ten pounds of nutmeg cost less than half a penny, ten pounds of mace was less than five pence. In Europe the prices were respectively £1.60 and £16. The canny new monarch would soon style himself "James, by the Grace of God King of England, Scotland, Ireland, France and Pulo Run." That last realm, thought one of its new visitors, might well contribute as much to the royal coffers as Scotland.

The local inhabitants were independent of any local sultan and largely unmolested by the Dutch. By 1616 they valued their English connection and surrendered themselves to the East India Company. The charter of 1600, however, never empowered the Company to hold overseas territories. Allegiance had to be accepted on behalf of the crown. Those two institutions, Company and crown, were to maintain a similarly strange division of power and authority for more than 200 years.

Of course, the crown was soon to take a little sabbatical and it was Oliver Cromwell who clarified the Company's powers by issuing a new charter allowing it to hold, fortify and settle overseas territory. Within half a century St Helena, Madras, Bombay, Calcutta and Bengal would be fortified and settled, though not always for profits to compete with nutmeg.

Poor old Pulo Run was not destined to rival such great places. In 1661, the same year that the Company took Bombay, Charles II ratified the Treaty of Breda, handing to the Dutch his possessions in the Banda Sea in return for important holdings in his Western Empire. The British swapped quiet, humble, sweet Pulo Run for other islands. They'd take Manhattan, the Bronx and Staten Island too.

BY 1667 and the publication of *Paradise Lost* Europe perceived the east and India as a source of opulence, decadence and tyranny, as Milton described in Book II:

> High on a throne of royal state, which far
> Outshone the wealth of Ormus and of Ind,
> Or where the gorgeous East with richest hand

> Showers on her kings barbaric pearl and gold,
> Satan exalted sat, by merit raised
> To that bad eminence.

That eminence didn't seem at all bad to the traders of the late seventeenth and the eighteenth centuries. The Portuguese had created an empire in the sub-continent throughout the sixteenth century to exploit their East Indies trade but also to worry the hated Ottoman Turks from the east of that infidel empire and to attempt the evangalisation of the Indians. Their great citadel, 'Golden' Goa, became an archbishopric and the Inquisition was established in 1560. This was an uncomfortable institution for Hindu and Muslim residents, even those well assimilated into Catholic society by the enlightened Portuguese policy of inter-marriage. The priesthood and the governors, converting and conquering, were brutal even for a savage age. The Portuguese were not loved in India and little missed when, as their native realm was subsumed into the greater Spanish monarchy, they lost their influence in the east.

Their empire survived in limited form more than four hundred years later. Goa, famous for its own aromatic herbal trade, would not be lost until 1961; while in distant Cathay, Macao, thriving on gambling, gold smuggling and prostitution, flew a Portuguese ensign over her derelict cathedral until the end of the twentieth century.

As in the Spice Isles, it was the Dutch who replaced the Portuguese in India. They had no imperial, missionary ambition, having emerged from the same Hapsburg autocracy that had taken the Lisbon government and directed its energy to the west. The Dutch did not want an empire; they wanted a monopoly. To exploit the wealth of their private spice trade, centred on Batavia, later called Jakarta, they needed complete control of the eastern trade routes. More importantly, they needed something to give to the islanders in return for those precious spices. Indian textiles were the accepted currency, and to buy textiles they needed silver. The Dutch set up an elaborate, intricate trading system in these three vital commodities, stretching from the Persian Gulf to Japan. Their objective was to buy cheap spice without releasing any resources from Europe and the home markets. This was the trade that bought the merchants of Delft and Amsterdam to Surat, Bengal, the Coromandel Coast at Negapatam and eventually right into Agra.

Like the Dutch, the English thought of India only as a source of cotton goods for the purchase of spice. In 1623, however, they were cruelly ousted from the Spice Isles by their Netherlandish rivals. The Dutch East India Company was far better organised, sponsored by the state, financed ten times better than the English, and manned by better informed, more expert navigators in faster, more heavily armed ships. The English East India Company finally withdrew from the East Indies only 23 years after its first adventure, after the horrible events at Amboina (now Ambon).

On the 9th of February, 1623 a Japanese employee of the Dutch Company was chatting idly to a guard on the parapets of Amboina, in the Banda Sea. His questions concerning the fort's defences alerted the suspicions of the guard. The man was arrested and tortured until he disclosed a fictional plan for mutiny in which the English were implicated. Fifteen Englishmen were living in the town by protection of a treaty. Their leader was Gabriel Towerson, one of the original Pulo Run crew 23 years before. They were summoned to the fort, obeyed as innocent men, and were chained in the dungeons or in the holds of the ships riding nearby.

The Dutch judge, the 'fiscal', was eager for confessions. The men were spread-eagled to a frame with their heads secured in the bottom of a canvas tube tied tightly at the neck:

> That done, they poured the water softly upon his head untill the cloth was full up to the mouth and nostrils and somewhat higher; so being poured in softly, forced all his inward partes to come out of his nose, eares and eyes; and often as it were stifling him, and at length took his breath away and brought him to a swoone or fainting.

After three or four such dunkings;

> ...his body was swollen twice or thrice as big as before, his cheeks like great bladders, and his eyes staring and strutting out beyond his forehead.

Clark, one of the factors, survived four of these douches before the Dutch held candles beneath his feet...

> untill the fat dropt and put out the candles. [They were relit and put to his chest] ...untill his innards might evidently be seene... Thus wearied and overcome by torment... [they all confessed except, perhaps, for Towerson.]

When Towerson was put before them to be denounced they almost all recanted those confessions at the sight of "That honest and godly man who harboured no ill will to anyone, much less attempt any such business as this." Ten of them were condemned to death, along with nine Japanese and one Portuguese. Towerson wrote his last letter signed " ...Gabriel Towerson, now appointed to dye, guiltless of anything that can be laid at my charge." The merchant's urge to strike a final deal was irresistible to one man on his way to the scaffold. He shouted: "If I be guilty, let me never partake of thye heavenly joyes, O Lord." "Amen for me, good Lord," cried all the others in turn.

The news of "this crying business of Amboina" was greeted with appalled shock in England. Some urged the Royal Navy to take the next Dutch ship in the Channel and have its crew "hung up upon the cliffs of Dover." Protests and complaints were made in Holland and James I reluctantly agreed to reprisals. Nothing was done. In 1625 a Dutch fleet bound for Batavia sailed through the Channel under the guns of the king's ships and the outraged Company subscribers decided that their governor, Sir Morris Abbot, might be a little too close to royal patronage. They withheld their subscriptions and urged the directors to "give over the trade of the Indies."

That trade was already ended. A small settlement buying pepper remained at Macassar until 1667, and at Bantam buying cloves until the 1680s. In policy and practice the British were out of the spice trade and reduced to their small possessions in India.

THE COMPANY had maintained links with the sub-continent since the early years of the century but the real breakthrough came when British forces defeated the

Portuguese at Swally in 1612. This great fight had the immediate, pleasing consequence of informing all interested parties that a new power had serious intentions in south Asia. More helpfully, it put the British in the good books of the big man in the region, Jehangir, Lord of the Mughal Empire and ruler of all the lands between Kabul and Bengal, Gujarat and Tibet, would now be pleased to welcome the Company's humble envoy.

He was particularly happy because the battle had removed a mild irritation. He had been concerned by the Portuguese command of those seaways necessary to his faithful subjects' *haj*, the holy pilgrimage to Mecca. He must have been overjoyed to find that his brother monarch had sent such an accomplished plenipotentiary as Sir Thomas Roe who brought the right gifts to please the luxurious potentate. He liked paintings "...espetially such as discover Venus' and Cupid's actes," and musical instruments. Roe provided a musician to play the emperor's new virginals, Lancelot Canning, a distant kinsman of India's future viceroy, whose performances were so badly received that he "dyed of conceitt."

The diplomatic dirty pictures worked. Roe's embassy, from 1615 to 1618, secured the emperor's *firman,* a grant of privileges by which the British secured the right to trade and establish factories in return for the Company's ships becoming an auxiliary navy for the Mughals. The British now had an economic interest in India and the sea power to defend it. The Amboina slaughter and Jehangir's *firman* ensured that the chief field of British activity in Asia would be India.

The British established posts at Hooghly (1641) in Bengal, and Masulipatam (1611) which was moved to Madras (1640) under the aegis of a Hindu raja before passing under the sultans of Golconda and then the Mughals (1687). They also traded through the independent city of Bombay, although the newly powerful Maratha stifled that town's economy by their control of the hinterland. The trade was different from that of the Dutch in that it depended on bulk, not rarity of goods. It did not need the armed force required by the Dutch to protect their monopoly. It relied on political goodwill rather than intimidation.

Like the Dutch, the British could only buy for silver. Like the Dutch, they created a complicated trading system to generate funds. Madras and Gujarat supplied cotton, Gujarat also provided indigo. Sugar, silk and saltpetre (for gunpowder) came from Bengal while a spice trade developed along the Malabar coast in direct rivalry to the Dutch. Opium was sent to China, eventually to generate an economy vital to British India. New textiles flowed from India back to Britain. As well as a rainbow of cottons, the British now wanted calicoes, taffetas, chintz and cashmere. All at once napkins and bed sheets and even underwear seemed quite indispensable. The Company's venture to enliven the dinner table revolutionised the boudoir.

In the 1680s the Company survived an attempt by the Glorious Revolutionaries to found a rival, eventually merging with the interloper under a new name: The United Company of Merchants Trading with the East Indies. The prevalent mercantilist philosophy, which abhorred the departure of bullion from Britain, proved a harder challenge. The mercantilists succeeded in making law in 1700, forbidding the sale of Asian silks and dyed or printed cotton in Britain. The Company survived by finding new cloth markets on the Continent for re-export and by developing the China tea trade.

While the French grew magic in their own vines and the Scots distilled sorcery in their own glens, the perverse English found their insipid national drink 18,000 miles away. Imports of the bitter little leaves increased from 54,000 pounds in 1706 to 2.3 million only 44 years later.

Robert Clive, conqueror of the Orient.

Warren Hastings, the first great British
administrator in India.

The Company courted potential disaster when its governor, Sir Josiah Child, decided to attempt war on the Great Mughal in Bengal. Child's War (1686-1690) might have been doomed. He chose to pick a fight with the greatest empire in Asia and an emperor with 100,000 men in the field. The governor of Bengal, the nawab, Shaista Khan, had 40,000 on the spot.

The British landed two companies of infantry; 308 men.

Disaster was prevented by the mutual confusion and mutual commercial skill of both sides. A Company fleet arrived at just the right moment to remind the nawab of the value of British bullion; 240,000 kilograms of silver and 7,000 kilograms of gold between 1681 and 1685. He also realised that the textiles exported to Britain were vital to Bengal's economy.

This persuasive accountancy was enhanced by the deceit of the British sailors who would leave the front to support the rear, giving the impression that their numbers were endless. The simple ploy was aided by the vast amounts of delightful marijuana based ghat that made battle such a lovely day out for the nawab's troops.

Commanding Company forces was Job Charnock, disdainful of his superiors and, most encouragingly for Anglo-Indian relations, of doubtful Christianity. He had found his wife, a young Hindu widow, by marching onto her husband's funeral pyre and dragging her into his arms in her smouldering sari.

He came to terms with the nawab in 1690 and demanded a new territorial concession. It had a good anchorage and fine land communications close to a village called Kalighat, named after Kali, Hindu goddess of destruction. Charnock honoured her by the name of his new town: Calcutta.

For the next half century the British prospered in India with no more than the occasional dispute over trading terms and rights at local level to cause friction with the Mughals. The Company's complete dominance of the sub-continent was to come, unbidden, from the coincidence of two great political sea-changes. The first was the original world war as France and Britain, nations a mere 22 miles apart, fought the Seven Years War two continents and two oceans from the Channel. The second was the repetition of an ancient story. The Mughal Empire, decadent, over-extended and with little central co-ordination, could resist neither the now terrifying strength of the Maratha nor the independence of its own princes. As the Caesars recruited Visi-Gothic legions to hold the Danube, the Mughals would seek the help of foreign arms. The question was; which set of foreigners would fill the vacuum? The British and the French were barbarians at the gate.

The French had never been much interested in global imperialism, preferring to weigh heavily their own scale in the delicate European balance of power. For most of the seventeenth century that balance had been measured on two pivots. The Bourbon sovereigns of France were destined to be at war with the Hapsburgs of Spain and Austria. Yet both those great dynasties were fated to fight the Protestant powers of Northern Europe. Europe was a mess from the end of the Thirty Years war in 1648 to the end of a tough afternoon for the Oriental Club's first and only president in 1815. Nevertheless, one of the comforting constants of history still prevailed; in India the British and the French managed to have their traditional fight.

In the Indian wars the French did not fight a nation of shopkeepers so much as attempt to steal the wholesaler's supplies. Their *Compagnie des Indes* was a comparative late comer, founded by Colbert in 1664. It bought Pondicherry, 85 miles south of Madras in 1674, and obtained Chandernagore, 16 miles north of Calcutta in 1690. The Dutch took Pondicherry in 1693, only to return it by treaty four years later with the best fortifications in India. By the middle of the next century France had Mahe in Malabar and Karikal on the east coast as well as the important shipping stage of Mauritius. Their trade was about half as valuable as the British; worth taking but no rival.

At the end of the War of Austrian Succession Joseph-Francoise, Marquis Depleix, governor of Pondicherry realised that another Franco-British war was inevitable, and that his cultivation of native power might not only secure the French position in India but also provide rich pickings for himself and his officials. He engineered the installation of his stooge, Chandra Sahib, as nawab of the Carnatic. The British in Madras could not allow this unbalanced influence so they soon sponsored their own nawab candidate, Muhammad Ali Khan. The two rivals were fighting a full-scale proxy war on behalf of the European powers by the late 1740s. In 1748 the French made a daring raid on Madras itself, only to be repulsed by the equal daring of a young, disgruntled, embittered Company clerk who revealed a much greater talent for battle than ever he had for book keeping.

Robert Clive was to become one of the two great architects of British India and, like his successor Warren Hastings, he would be disappointed, even betrayed by his compatriots at home.

The war in the Carnatic stumbled on inconclusively for five years during which both sides increasingly used native troops, sepoys, trained in European warfare. Both sides imported troops from home, although Indian service was not then popular with European soldiers. Robert Orme, a Company officer, described the new recruits landing at Madras in 1752 as "the refuse of the vilest employments in London."

The Carnatic was not to be the testing ground for Britain. In 1756 Calcutta was taken by the new nawab of Bengal, Siraj-ud-Daula, in response to Britain's growing military power in the region and her merchants' rapacious exploitation of privileges taken by force. Prestige was missed more than revenue, especially as the governor and his entourage ran away to leave the survivors to a cruel fate. The Bengalis mocked the British *banchots,* cowards, and locked them in the local detention cell at Fort William. Perhaps as many as 140 people spent the night in a room 18 feet by 15, deprived of water, gasping for air. There were many deaths, but the Black Hole was not an unusually cruel barbarity. Its significance was the creation of Zephania Holwell, one of the 23 survivors, whose emotive account of his night in the cell, of fights for the window space, the drinking of sweat and urine and the dead falling beneath the weight of their comrades, would create an uproar to rival that of Amboina.

The Black Hole itself did not enter the mythology for some years; the short term response to the loss of Calcutta was more important. Eventually that hard night at Fort William would propel the propaganda that British people were bound to civilise Indian people, with no further judgement required. As the historian Nirad Chaudhuri observed, it "threw a moral halo over the British conquest of India." In fact Holwell's account unwittingly reveals how ignobly the British behaved towards each other in an emergency.

Clive moved quickly, abandoning Carnatic operations against the French to march on Bengal. He had many advantages, the greatest being the venality and corruption of Shiraj's court. The nawab was advised by courtesans and catamites, defended by solders of little loyalty and supported by bankers who admired safe profit more than fidelity, as is the characteristic of their usurious profession.

After easily relieving Calcutta in January, 1757, Clive bought off Mir Jafir, the nawab's army commander, and enticed the Seth banking clan to join him against their old client. Politically and financially destroyed, the last independent nawab of Bengal met the muskets of the Company at Plassey on the 23rd of June, 1757.

The battle seemed unequal. Clive had 1,000 Europeans, and 2,000 sepoys supported by eight small cannon and one howitzer. Shiraj had at least 50,000 cavalry and infantry and a large artillery train drawn by bullocks. But the nawab's great host was loose and riven by treachery, Mir Jafir kept his men shy of the fight and those who did stand were unnerved by the rapidity of British trained volleys and close-range bombardment. The British cannon aimed for the bullocks which stampeded in terror across the Bengali ranks. Clive himself led the offence which made his army like a tiger, writes Chaudhuri, "who never charges if he can scatter his enemy with a roar."

The nawab was soon taken and murdered by Mir Jafir's servants. The Company had defeated an army of 50,000 for the loss of 73 killed and wounded.

This was easy work. After Plassey, Clive became the North Indian kingmaker, with all those kings dependent upon the Company for their position and power if not their authority. Clive made Mir Jafir nawab of Bengal, Orissa and Bihar. All land tax passed directly to the Company, as did justice and policing in 1772. The French were expelled from Bengal and the new revenue used to continue the fight in the Carnatic. Pondicherry was razed in 1761 although, by the Treaty of Paris which ended the Seven Years War in Europe, the land was returned to the French.

The British were no longer mere traders, sometimes welcome, usually tolerated. They were now the most powerful political, economic and military force in India. Merchants had become soldiers: and conquest was clearly much more rewarding than trade. The Company, known now as the *Bahadur*, the honourable or valiant Company, would make men rich by taxation and booty. More destructively even than this, the British learned to expect wealth by corruption.

After 20 years of conquest and pacification Edmund Burke told the House of Commons in 1785 that,

> The great fortunes made in India at the beginnings of the conquest naturally excited emulation in all parts and through the whole succession of the Company's servants.

They were not slow to emulate. Giving gifts was, as Clive said, "the known and usual custom of Eastern princes." He gratefully received £234,000 from Mir Jafir between 1757 and 1766, and other officials graciously accepted gifts of between £5,000 and £117,000. Influence was a purchasable commodity in eighteenth century India, as it was in eighteenth century Britain, and the influential saw no reason to break with accepted tradition.

If the fruits of conquest were attractive, the fruits of war were irresistible. As a junior officer before 1753 Clive made £40,000 in prize money. A later, more senior and much more scrupulous soldier, one Colonel Arthur Wellesley, brought home £43,000 from his Indian tour of 1798 to 1805; more than he would ever make commanding at Waterloo. With such treasure so tantalisingly close, the young officers of the Company were understandably eager for war, writing home of their distress at cancelled campaigns. One subaltern at Madras described his comrades in 1797:

> Judge of the gloom, the disappointment, and vexation which overspread the faces which a few moments before had exhibited the highest symptoms of hope, and ardour for distinction.

He was of the first generation that might one day exchange nostalgic tales over a glass in Hanover Square. Those, that is, who survived. John Malcolm, when a very junior officer, could live fairly high even without much glorious booty and, unusually and creditably, without corruption. He entered the Company service in 1781, had accumulated £13,000 23 years later and still managed to send an annual £400 to his grateful parents and sisters in their damp bothy. When he left the service in 1806 he had sufficient capital to provide an income of £1,500 a year, a fortune in itself.

By 1800 a commission in the Company's army was a valuable asset to any middle class boy. Unable to afford the private income required to support a junior officer in the king's service, a man could find a gentlemanly occupation that paid its way, sometimes in rubies. Envy, rather than glory, led the officers of the crown to look disdainfully on the Company's men.

The founding chairman of the Oriental Club exhibited another characteristic of his age. The desire for lucrative fighting created a bellicose culture in India and in the gasping population back at home. When a Company director interviewed the twelve-year-old John Malcolm in 1781 he asked "Why, little man, what would you do if you were to meet Hyda Ali?" "Do, Sir?" exclaimed the wee bairn, "I would out with my sword and cut off his head," or so Malcolm told the story in his memoirs. Whatever the truth, it was enough to get him his precocious commission in the Company force.

THE VICTORIAN historian Sir John Seeley noted in his work *The Expansion of England* that;

> We the English seem, as it were, to have conquered and peopled half the world in a fit of absence of mind.

The London governments of the late eighteenth century had no policy of eastern empire, had not striven for India and seemed rather surprised to find the union flag flying over a civilisation that made the average squire in the Commons seem like a semi-literate savage. Some of those stay-at-home squires might also have felt unfairly poor as the wealth of India was unloaded at the Company docks in Deptford. The reaction of this most venal political establishment was to censure the great leaders of British enterprise in India. The charge of corruption might have held more than a grain of truth but few pots have had such shameless temerity toward a kettle.

Robert Clive had returned for a second tenure as governor of Bengal in 1765. He was a reformer, obtaining for the Company the full suzerainty of the province under the impotent Mughal authority, founding a pension fund for disabled officers and creating a system of government which encouraged mutual respect between Indians and British. His dual system allowed the Company to collect tax as the emperor's agent, his dewan, while administration remained in Indian hands under a Company appointed deputy. For this job Clive selected the Persian officer Muhammad Riza Khan, whose own later show trial found him innocent of corruption. The puppet nawabs after Mir Jafir retained their regalia but no army and no money without application to the Company.

Within the Company, Clive ensured that gifts of more than 1,000 rupees were to be accepted only with the governor's consent and that any present greater than 4,000 rupees was forbidden. Of course, he created enemies; defeating a mutinous brigade commander in a duel, enforcing resignations and failing only to regulate the private trade that so enriched those natural merchants left in the Company. He recognised his own earlier sins, remarking that;

> In a country where money is plenty, where fear is the principle of government, and when your arms are ever victorious, I say it is no wonder that corruption should find its way to a spot so well prepared to receive it.

He did all in his power to stamp it out.

When he returned to London in 1767 his enemies soon found ammunition to hunt him through Parliament; for he had held a seat in the Commons and was now a peer. He was entirely vindicated in 1773. Always melancholic and addicted to opium, Clive had attempted suicide as a youth. In 1774 the victor of Plassey, conqueror of Bengal and saviour of the East India Company was utterly justified but unjustly hounded. He sat down by a chilly fireside as either he or, as was later rumoured, his wife took out a knife and opened his throat. He was 49 years old.

Two years previously the Company had sent out a new governor of Bengal; another reformer and incorruptible. Warren Hastings' rule was bedevilled by the culture of bribery among his subordinates, opposition from his own council, hostility from the British government and lack of support from Company headquarters in Leadenhall Street. In his 13 years in Bengal he managed to create an equitable system of justice despite the ignorance of British judges of Persian or Urdu, the languages traditionally used in court. He never had quite the authority to defeat his enemies within the Company, particularly Sir Philip Francis, a member of his council in Calcutta, ardent supporter of venality and sometime duelling opponent. Hastings' achievements were ignored on his return to Britain, but he was blamed for all those faults he had fought against. It is true that he was harsh towards Raja Chait Singh of Varanasi and the baygums, princesses, of Oudh, but he needed their resources to compensate for the Company money falling into private pockets.

Were it not for his loyalty both to the crown and the Company, Hastings might now be celebrated as the father of his nation. He resisted serious moves for some sort of United States of Bengal and Madras. The British in India suffered similar frustrations and deprivations by the home government as their counterparts in North America. Hastings deflated a small movement for a declaration of independence, more faithful to the Company charter than Colonel Washington was to his commission in the militia of the king's colony of Virginia.

Hastings was impeached in Parliament in 1787. Proceedings lasted for eight years before he walked from Westminster Hall entirely cleared after a trial lasting 145 days. The accusations were instigated by Edmund Burke and the Whigs for noble but ignorant reasons. They were appalled at the wealth and violence, as well as the corruption of the Company. The playwright Richard Brinsley Sheridan, one of Burke's closest allies in the Commons described the accepted view:

> They send all their troops to drain the products of industry, to seize all the treasures, wealth and prosperity of the country. Like a vulture with their harpy talons grappled in the vitals of the land, they flap away the lesser kites and they call it protection. It is the protection of the vultures to the lamb.

Tippu Sultan, the Tiger of Mysore and the first tyrant destroyed by Wellington.

The club's Mather Brown shows Tippu suspiciously cheeful as he delivers his
sons as hostages to Cornwallis.

They served notice that the Company's servants were responsible to those they governed in India, and answerable to Parliament for that government. Hastings was so closely associated with the piratical government of British India that he became the inevitable target for such declarations of principle. Sheridan went on to describe Hastings:

> His crimes are the only great things about him, and these are contrasted by the littleness of his motives. He is at once a tyrant, a trickster, a visionary and a deceiver ...he reasons in bombast, prevaricates in metaphor and prevaricates in heroics.

In fact, they got quite the wrong man.

Hastings was a little more phlegmatic than his predecessor, retiring to the family estate at Daylesford to die, duly honoured, in 1818. His vigorous governance had persuaded the British government that it had a responsibility in India. That obligation was recognised in William Pitt's India Act of 1784. Indians and British were to enjoy the same law, now English law. The directors of the Company were to answer to a Board of Control, originally headed by Henry Dundas as minister for India. The governor-general in Calcutta would supervise all the British holdings in India, aided by a council of three, including the commander-in-chief, over whom he now had the veto so much missed by Hastings. The Company's independence was reduced by the renewal clause; the charter would be renewed every 20 years only if it satisfied a Parliamentary committee of enquiry.

The structure of Indian administration was set for the next 70 years. The British in the east were intent on putting more and more of India under that administration. THE OFFICIAL Company policy after Clive's conquests was that no further territorial expansion should be sought; the Company was still in commerce not government. Few in India took much notice of such an asinine direction from Leadenhall Street. The British were as eager for martial riches as ever; the Indian states were as keen for their arms; and non-aligned territories might still be a danger, or even look to France.

When the Duke of Wellington died in 1852 The Times obituarist wrote that he,

> ...has exhausted nature and exhausted glory. His career was one unclouded longest day.

Napoleon Bonaparte was clearly the most important man in the making of that career, giving the duke triumphs in the Peninsula and in person near Brussels that made him like a Perecles or a Pompey (Wellington would have hated the allusion: "Don't quote Latin; say what you want to say and then sit down," he once advised a new member of Parliament). Before such moments could be won, however, Arthur Wellesley needed the help of his big brother for his position and a brave, crazy sultan for his first great victory.

The powerful Hindu kingdom of Mysore, outside the authority or protection of the withering Mughal empire, had been taken over by a brilliant, Muslim thief of nations in 1762. Hyda Ali Khan, the man who excited such aggressive instincts in the young John Malcolm, was as tolerant a ruler as he was a magnificent general. His rule was resented by his subjects, but that resentment was tempered by the gentleness with which he treated the usurped dynasty and the security to which he bought his stolen realm.

He died 20 years later "of a carbuncle in the district now called North Arcot," according to a Colonel Love, or "of a boil upon his back," according to the Madras council. He was succeeded by an heir with all his brilliance but little of his judgement. Tippu Sultan was bound by various treaties to support the aggressive policy against Madras of the Marathi and the unstable Nizam of the Deccan. He would have been trouble anyway; he was a man made of mischief. Tippu, 'the Tiger of Mysore', had a favourite toy, the man-tiger-organ, which caused great interest when it was installed at the Company's museum in Leadenhall Street in 1808, so much so that it was the inspiration for John Keats' fairy-tale *The Cap and Bells*. It was a life-size mechanical tiger disembowelling a Company officer, the growls of the cat and the groans of the captain faithfully reproduced by an internal barrel organ (it is now in the Victoria and Albert Museum, though much damaged in the blitz). Such was the sultan's sense of fun; he frequently enjoyed this little tableau performed for real in the frighteningly feline courtyard of his citadel at Seringapatam.

Tippu had an even better toy in Mysore itself. He mobilised his realm in the European way. In 1791, according to Admiralty intelligence, his agents in Paris procured 50 cannon, 80 gun carriages, 100,000 cannon shot, 10,000 muskets and 20,000 'best tempered sabres'. The tiger clearly meant business, even if he might have had the raw end of a deal on 30 spare gun carriages. His claws were drawn in 1792 with much effort by Lord Cornwallis, a commander still smarting from his defeat by Colonel Washington (then known by the dubious title of 'general' within his own treacherous rebel band) at Yorktown a decade before. Tippu's first brush with the British gave John Malcolm his chance to shine.

In the rich wall sized canvas that hangs in the club, Mather Brown depicts a delighted, beaming sultan commending his sons to the care of jolly uncle Cornwallis. The second elephant from the right has a quizzical slant to his eyebrow that suggests that the wise old beast knew better: Tippu was furious. He might have known that the children were safe in the hands of the fat fellow in red but, like a fairy tale king, he also had to hand over half his kingdom.

He had ordered a new throne, a vast construction of platforms and canopies around the central divan, all decorated with his increasingly obsessive motif of tigers. Now he vowed never to mount this stripy seat until he had regained his losses and defeated the British.

Comforting historical constants prevailed. Whenever princes have resolved to defeat the British they have rarely failed to find an ally in the French. Tippu dealt with a new revolutionary regime in Paris and gained arms, training and a professional general staff. By the time the final battle was fought those patient French officers were to hold the sultan in their respect, affection and exasperation in equal measure.

Concepts like liberty, egality and fraternity were about as familiar to the politics of India as runny cheese and unfeasibly long bicycle races. Nevertheless, the sultan let it be known that he was now 'Citizen Tippu', although his subjects became no more familiar with the rights of man. In fact Tippu was no tyrant. He was merciless to political opponents but he was no greater burden to the people of Mysore than his predecessors. He was simply absurd, wearing the Phrygian cap of liberty over a turban as his tigers strolled the palace parks.

He was, however, a worthy enemy for the British. They had a worthy governor-general. The Marquis Wellesley took office in 1798, accompanied by his young brother Arthur in command of a battalion of the 33rd Regiment of Foot. This was not the first unit of king's soldiers to assist the British in India by half a century, but it was among one of the biggest detachments to be sent by a newly responsible government to march with the Company forces.

The Marquis was passionately opposed to the French Revolution; for some reason he found the French even more obnoxious under a republic than he had under the kings his nation had been fighting for centuries. Perhaps, being a marquis, if only a first marquis, he objected to a government with a creditable record of aristocratic decapitation. More alarming was the presence of a French army in Egypt, cut off from home by Nelson's victory on the Nile and led by an ambitious young General Bonaparte who might have been tempted to emulate Alexander and march from the delta to the Indus. Wellesley had no patience for the Francophile sultan and his Jacobin officers; his policy was to secure the sub-continent for British power. The army marched on Mysore in 1799 under General Harris, with Colonel Wellesley second in command. Tippu was not weak, but he was not strengthened by the traditional treachery within his high command, though those who were not loyal were not necessarily real traitors: they worked for a restoration of the old Hindu dynasty. The 30-year-old Wellesley took a leading part in the long siege and a crucial part in the final assault of Serangapatam. Having taken a colonelcy by patronage, he now took one of the greatest fortresses of Asia by splendour of arms. The future first and only president of the Oriental Club was now given the governorship of the fallen city along with his first laurels.

Tippu died among his men in the tough street fighting that followed the breach of the walls. The famous scene of Company officers finding his body that night was often used to illustrate the triumph of British arms over Eastern despotism. His heavily bejewelled scimitar was soon looted but the many wounds left by bayonets twisted in his body suggest that the sword remained in his hand to the last. That famous scene also illustrates the mortal courage of a prince who finally knew that he would never mount the tiger throne.

He was buried in his parents' mausoleum, the *Gumbaz*, where his tomb is covered by a cloth of tiger stripes.

The Wellesley boys soon cleared up the rest of Southern India. The older brother secured the alliance and effective control of the Mahrathi over-lord, the Peshwa, master of a nation devastated by its long, mutually destructive struggle against the Mughal power. In 1803 the resistant armies of Gwailor and Nagpur were defeated by little Arthur, now major-general, at Assaye and Argaon. In the north General Sir Gerrard Lake took Aligarh, Delhi and Agra. A final Marathi prince was too much for the marquis: Jaswant Rao Holkar gave Sir Gerrard a bad time at Baratpur and a Company column was deeply uncomfortable near Agra in 1805.

The Marquis Wellesley was recalled the next year, presumably concerned that his family name might be deeply tarnished. He was a proud and arrogant man, so much so that his junior officers would tell the tale that he wore his decorations on his night-shirt. Wellesley had ruled as a patrician pro-consul: in Cawnpore in 1802 he had ridden an elephant in;

...the true style of Eastern pomp, distributed his [the Company's] rupees with a liberal hand, just like an Indian potentate.

He had little time for the accountants of Leadenhall Street. They were, he wrote in 1799;

> ...held in universal contempt and ridicule in every branch of the service in India.

The divided interests in India were already appearing. Arthur thought his older brother's policy extended lines too far; Leadenhall Street realised that, for all its authority, the Company was making less money out of India than its employees. The governors, solders and merchants no longer had a common cause.

That division of motives was soon replaced by a strange coalition of ideas which were practically hypocritical but ideologically generous. The young General Arthur Wellesley had no problems hanging Indians without trial, condemning "liberal ideas" from Britain. Having strung up Magna Carta with one hand he saluted British fair play with the other: he wrote to John Malcolm in 1804 that

> I would rather sacrifice Gwailor or every other frontier in India ten times over, in order to preserve our credit for scrupulous good faith.

Malcolm had the same trust in British good faith, without its cruelty, but he had learned by experience as the marquis's secretary that the princes of India might not return such faith. The British must assert themselves by force of arms, he wrote:

> When they condescend to meet the smooth tongued Mohammedan, or the crafty Hindoo, with the weapons of flattery, dissimulation and cunning, they will to a certainty be vanquished.

It should not reflect upon the club they founded that the first chairman and the first and only president were the begetters of chauvinism. With the political, economic and military superiority of India, the British soon presumed their moral superiority.

The marquis begot a more tangible remembrance of his rule in India: his bastard son Gerald joined the Bengal Civil Service in 1807 and the Oriental Club in 1833.

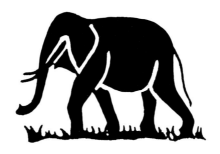

Chapter III

Crises

THE ANCIENT Iron Duke was a frequent visitor to the Great Exhibition of 1851. He, like the rest of Victoria's subjects, spent the year celebrating the variety, wealth and ingenuity of an empire at its height. The makers of that empire could afford a complacent, proud smile as they passed the Crystal Palace on their way to a comforting drink of China tea, Malacca coffee or Bombay gin, served in the comfort of a club in Hanover Square.

Their complacency was short-lived. When India mutinied in 1857 the membership of the club was appalled. The committee received a few lame excuses for failure to pay subscriptions, all quickly dismissed by men who well knew the special financial arrangements made by India House to look after the dispossessed, but the members did all they could to help their beleaguered colleagues out east. Appeals were set up for an India Famine Relief Fund in 1861, another in 1877, and for the wreck survivors of Her Majesty's Ships Bombay and Racehorse in 1865. The first had burned off Montevideo, the second foundered on the China route. Lloyd's of London reports that she was

...wrecked in the China Seas about five leagues south-east of Chefoo Cape. The ship's company were sent aft, and told that if they held on till daylight there was every hope of all hands being saved. But the poor fellows dropped off one by one from the effect of the cold and the force of the sea. Only nine were saved.

The club's charity extended to others hurt by a weakness in Imperial trade. The Distressed Lancashire Operatives' Fund (1862) supported those distressed by the fall off in cotton manufacturing caused by 'the unpleasantness between the States', the self-destructive civil war fought by the successors of treacherous Colonel Washington.

Strangely, the club was untypically mean to a cause that should have been close to members' hearts. The minutes record a collecting box for the 'Sufferers of the land-slip at Naini Tal', started on the 26th of October, 1880, and ended three weeks later because there were "no subscribers."

Usually generous, the early members of the club would occasionally find themselves suffering more local land-slips. They used to fall over a lot. Mr Wilton had "partly destroyed" 14 chairs "by his infirmities" in 1834. Later such delicate excuses were less well forgiven. Complaints to the committee included:

> Captain F: Filing his nails during breakfast.
> Mr G P: Wearing the club bath slippers in the coffee room.
> Mr G: Scraping toast on the coffee room floor.
> Dr W: Drinking ale and using a fork in the drawing room.
> Anon : Entering the strangers room in flannels and a cap.
> Mr C F: Reading aloud to himself in the library.
> Several : Spitting, throat clearing and the like in a variety of contexts.
> Several : Snoring.

It was a tough regime that forbade a man from clearing his throat in a variety of contexts, and even tougher that he had to scrape his toast on the coffee room floor. Snoring, of course, was to become an afternoon tradition.

Some heinous behaviour had to be tolerated. Members were ceaselessly reminded that they may not put their feet up on the sofas. The committees were deeply distressed by this felony and instructed the staff to chastise offenders. Time after time they were "shown the relevant notice" until grown men who had seen the luxuries of Bombay and Kuala Lumpur despaired. "What are sofas for?" wrote Mr Courtenay, "except to put you feet on." No committee mentioned the subject again and the couches of the club would welcome a reclining member .

One of the original debenture members, Captain E A Trevor of the Royal Artillery disliked stockinged feet. He wrote to the chairman in 1875:

> Sir,
>
> I would draw your attention to the fact that I saw one of the members, Mr Payter, sitting in the Smoking Room of the Club with his boots off - an act I consider filthy and ungentlemanly. A member of the Conservative Club noticed it, and I fear that he left the Oriental Club with an erroneous impression of its character and tone.
>
> I have the honour to be, Sir...

Field Marshal the Duke of Wellington, Duke Arthur, first and only president of the
Oriental Club.

Oriental members would always have to look around before slipping off a shoe under the table. The Conservative Club, having been subsumed by many amalgamations, would eventually unite with the Bath Club which, in turn, united with the Oriental in the 1970s.

Gambling, however, has always been encouraged, on the form of horses and the fall of cards. Cards, regrettably, were unwelcome at the club in the 1860s. The culprit, as is so often the case in these matters, was a clergyman of the Church of England.

The Reverend J. O. Oldham played too high and at completely the wrong time of year. He started a game one evening that did not end before seven the next morning. It is surely to the credit of the club, but to the disappointment of his parishioners, that he started play on the evening of Christmas Day, 1862, and was of little use as a preacher on Boxing Day. His resignation would have been requested had so many of the committee not been in the country for Christmas. The Reverend Mr Oldham replied to the committee's repeated complaints with his own: the club's anchovies, apparently, were never quite to his satisfaction. He founded a school that played beyond eight in the morning in July, 1867, and beyond half-past-three in the morning on the successive Saturdays and Sundays.

Joyless and intolerant, the sufficient committee members now assembled to ask for the holy man's resignation. He was not happy, writing that they;

> ...made a spectacle not only to the members of the Club, but to menials of the same ...severed from the circle of my friends ...publicly disgraced and a stigma attached to my name.

The club should have enjoyed the cloth when it could. Christianity, far harsher than the Hinduism and Islam familiar to most members, struck hard in Hanover Square. In keeping with the evangelical imperialism of the middle of the century, many members returned from India devoted to a missionary position. The committee had to take it lying down when James Farish came back to England and complained that the sporting members of the club were holding a horse racing lottery. In July, 1844, he pointed out that such wagers were contrary to rule 43 of the Oriental Club. The committee played for time and suggested he bring the matter up before the annual general meeting. In November Farish put before the committee an opinion by the solicitor-general which advised that such lotteries were illegal. The committee was unimpressed. Mr Farish resigned the next March.

In July the Court of Common Pleas heard *Allport v. Nutt* and found that racing lotteries were indeed illegal. The committee, much chagrined, enquired whether the odious Mr Farish would welcome back his membership. He returned. Members stopped wagering on the ponies within their own club.

Farish continued to proselytise: in 1849 he failed to persuade the committee that the club should take the *Church Missionary Intelligencer* and in 1850 he donated to the library *Wilson's Sermons on the Sabbath*. He never was popular for buying a round. The minutes of 1873 tell a bitter but sweetly mortal story:

> 13, February: The death of Mr Farish was reported.
> 8, April: An annual sweep on the Derby was sanctioned.

Perhaps Farish had a point about card playing, conscious as he was of a scandal involving the club a few years before his own return. *The Times* reports a Chancery case of 1843, *Osbaldeston v Simpson and Others*, which put the club to public scrutiny and censure. George Osbaldeston won very heavily from a member, a Mr Bowles, who paid £700 in cash and £2,100 in IOUs. Later, at the club and in the presence of Henry Simpson and, perhaps, a loquacious bottle, Osbaldeston is alleged to have confessed to cheating. He had apparently introduced a pack of marked cards.

The outraged Bowles was not too outraged to look up the law and find that, by an old law ("a statute of Queen Anne"), the cheat owed the cheated three times his fraudulent winnings; being £8,400. Yet they were gentlemen, of course, and so Osbaldeston agreed to pay Bowles £9,000, by promissory note, if he agreed to keep the whole thing quiet.

Inevitably, Bowles revealed the cheat's dark secret, the cheat failed to honour his promissory note; and the whole sad affair was publicly adduced in evidence during Osbaldeston's action against Simpson, Bowles and another witness to the alleged confession, Mr Chinery, also an Oriental. Osbaldeston's application was for an injunction preventing the others from suing him on his notes. The vice-chancellor granted it, holding that they may not bring their own action against Osbaldeston to honour promissory notes obtained by extortion.

Thus the English law took a characteristically confused attitude to justice and fair play and the Oriental Club gained a brief and pleasingly roguish notoriety as a den of card-sharps and blackmailers.

Osbaldeston himself was a famous master of fox hounds, jockey, boxer, theatrical impresario and sometime member of Parliament, known throughout the realm as the "Squire of England." It is very unlikely that he really had cheated, he had no need to, and so the committee expelled Bowles unanimously and without debate. Osbaldeston had already had one, potentially lethal confrontation with a member of the club. Lord William Bentink, a future governor-general of India, and his nephew Lord George Bentink were both original members. George, as well as being the leader of the opposition in the Commons to Peel's cruel Corn Law, was the most prominent breeder and jockey of his day. It was gambling, naturally, that brought him to "eat grass before breakfast" with Osbaldeston; a dawn duel in Hyde Park. Both walked away from the meeting in 1831 reasonably intact and, presumably, with honours even and satisfied.

Osbaldeston's gambling sums at the club are instructive. The loss of more than £3,000 in one night's gaming must be unusual for most members in the late twentieth century. The same treasure in the 1840s would be worth more than a hundred times that in 1998 money. Even if reckless members were playing with their whole fortunes, such a game, honest or not, demonstrates the wealth still bought back from the east; the fruitfulness of the pagoda tree.

Nevertheless, members did not tend to play very high. Cards were for the benefit of social occupation rather than adrenaline or bank accounts. Only one other serious incident was reported to the committee. The minutes of September, 1835 record that a game played by Mr Lutyens and Mr Lewis got out of control: there was "extreme violence of conduct and language", and the traditional, sometimes deadly demand for satisfaction was made. Witnesses testified to raw words. "You are an impudent fellow," shouted Lewis, not a man of devastating invective. Lutyens tried to hit him. Lewis picked up a bottle, smashed the glass ragged and threatened to use it in bloody savagery. By-standers intervened and violence was averted. Lutyens resigned, whether in shame or complaint is not recorded, and Lewis apologised to a committee that wisely took the matter no further.

Violence was mercifully rare among the members, mostly proud men in a duelling age. The absence of women from the club doubtless removed the usual cause of competition; and the membership were not young men. Yet mad, unprovoked, sober-craziness must dance in men's minds from time to time. One lunchtime in November, 1841, Dr Bucke was enjoying a solitary meal, quietly keeping himself to himself, when another member, who he did not recognise and to whom he had never spoken, marched up to his table, threw a jug of water in his face and declared "Take that. You have insulted me deliberately." The mad aggressor was Dr Wyllie, who was later firmly informed by the secretary that steps had been taken to safeguard for other members "the quiet and protection from personal violence which they have a right to expect." Wyllie maintained that he had been insulted, "premeditatedly, without provocation, insulted."

The incident might have no explanation other than a random release of unspecific wrath. Yet Bucke might have been disingenuous in claiming not to recognise his attacker. Both doctors had served with the Indian Medical Service in Madras at about the same time; perhaps some ancient diagnostic dispute may never have been forgiven. Whatever the truth, the protagonists never again drew the committee's attention.

The normal behaviour of the Victorians in the Oriental club was, if not sober, then quiet and restrained, although Sir John Kaye's description of "the traditional moroseness of the retired nabob" was unfair and anachronistic. Cruel but more accurate was a journalist of *The New Monthly Magazine* in 1843, describing those returned from the east as

...gentlemen who have passed the bloom of life in the money-making regions of Bundlecund and Ferruckabad and who, like Rosina's morning, 'return in saffron dressed'... They feed chiefly on curry and drink Madeira.

Rarely dressed in saffron, Victorian members found their club full of curry, comfort and companionship. Perhaps William Thackeray was right, in one of his many references to the club, when he said that the Oriental was the dullest club in London. That is what the members wanted. They had no journalistic need to invent a Ferruckabad or a Bundlecund; they had lived in real, distant places more fantastic than the imaginations of most members of more lively clubs. Like their founders, they wanted the simple luxury to remember maharajas.

By the end of the nineteenth century, a year before the end of the reign, the Victorians in the Oriental had created a conservative, slightly complacent club. After the condescension of the evangelists in the middle of the century and the horror of the Mutiny, a new generation was returning from India, trained under Lord Curzon, a viceroy almost as respectful of Indians and as generous in government as the Marquis Wellesley, and even more personally arrogant. Within a few years would come Ypres and Amritsar, but when Victoria died the members could already look back on a history covering three quarters of a century and forming a generous but specific identity to their club.

Of course, the magnificent Alexander Baillie recorded that history with unrivalled brilliance and charm in 1901.

The older members then, those who might remember the high living of the Regency, had habits that seemed delightfully louche to the later Victorians. In the

Buddha watches over a welcoming haven in the front lobby.

last year of the queen's reign Baillie wrote of his predecessors with undisguised envy:

> ...several gentlemen only wear a stock or scarf of many colours folded several times round the throat; and their hats - their hats are of real beaver, broad at the top and in the brim, and low in the crown. They jingle their spurs, they strike their boots with their hand-canes; they take snuff, and call for beer, and they swear! how they do swear!

Almost certainly, they were not wearing only a stock or scarf, whatever else was made of real beaver.

Baillie goes on to remember two brothers, both members, both colonels in the Company service, both very old when he was very young:

> They were not only on very friendly terms, but between them there was a real affection, and yet they never met, never saluted one another, without a strong expletive, not to say a curse, upon their lips. It meant absolutely nothing, but they followed what had been the fashion in the days of the Regency and of George IV.

Expletives and curses in the time of the Regency and George IV would not have been too shocking. 'Wipe my eye' or 'kiss my hand' would have been far too strong for Jane Austen, although brother Company colonels might have requested the decorous, stove-pipe wearing members of the late nineteenth century to kiss them elsewhere.

Such men, the companions of Wellington and Malcolm, were well within living memory when Victoria died, and still part of the living culture of the club. The membership and its personality were well defined and intact but, by the time Baillie wrote, it was close to a miracle that the Oriental Club still existed, such had been its trials.

SIR JOHN Malcolm did all he could to ease the life of members when he founded the Oriental Club in 1824. Within his titanic vision had been the need for a secretary so, before the club had even moved to Hanover Square in 1828, he had appointed Thomas Cornish to that office. Malcolm was beloved of shahs and field marshals but even a man of his vast intelligence and experience could make mistakes. Cornish would turn out to be a big mistake.

The chairman of the Oriental Club 14 years later, in 1842, was Sir Herbert Compton, soldier, journalist, barrister and ex-Chief Justice of Bombay. He was 72 years old, wily and wise - as indeed he had to be to maintain order at the committee meeting called at the secretary's request on the 10th of October. The secretary did not turn up. A servant was sent to his house on Marlborough Street but Cornish could not be found.

Compton had the committee meet again two days later when he revealed to them the contents of the letter he had received that morning in the spidery hand of the Oriental Club's first secretary:

Sir,

Pecuniary embarrassments have of late pressed so heavily upon me that I have been unable to stand up against them. Each hope I entertained, and I had many well-founded ones, has failed me, and I am in the position of having failed in the trust reposed in me by the club. To meet yourself, Sir, and the other gentlemen of the club with my present feelings is impossible, and I have quitted London...

Poor, sad Tom Cornish had done a runner. Worse, he had taken the club's money. He bestowed on the club a deficit of £2,635, 11 shillings and 7 pennies. This was a bad time to steal from the Oriental: subscriptions and trading receipts were badly down that year. By the end of 1842 the club had liabilities of £4,400 with only £889 and 10 shillings in the bank.

Having contracted to "give up the whole of his time to the service of the club, and not to hold any other situation" Cornish had for years been a partner in a print selling enterprise with a rascally Mr Laver. The business had been failing for a long time but survived as Cornish steadily propped it up with the club's money, paying his creditors at the end of the year with subscriptions owed to the club for the next year. All other bills he delayed paying until after the club's annual general meeting in May and then pilfered from the club accounts. In deceit, if not scale, it was an embezzlement of Maxwellian proportion and, of course, the fraud was always going to tumble down.

The Oriental Club was in grave danger. Compton, happily, was just the man to save it. Even a club riddled with generals and admirals could occasionally appreciate a lawyer's mind.

The club was Cornish's major creditor but other creditors competed. Mr Laver himself demanded the prints and other stock he had jointly owned with Cornish. The club maintained its claim. News got worse. On the 14th of November the club's solicitor advised the committee that little or nothing could be recovered from the fugitive secretary. Compton retained the composure to move the committee's resolution to thank a Dr Moore for the gift of some pickled mangoes.

A month later the worst of news arrived. Cornish had £6,000 claimed against him by creditors quite apart from the club. To the committee's naive astonishment, he had forged a cheque in a member's name for £300. Then, surely to no one's surprise, it was discovered that he had fled to the United States, that nation led to a spurious independence by the treacherous Colonel Washington.

The Federal Department of Immigration has no record of the arrival of Thomas Cornish in 1842 or 1843. These were days a few years before the Irish were starved across the ocean, before Ellis Island and before beaurocracy had assumed its fully terrifying shape in America, but it is likely that Cornish either never made the crossing, died at sea or changed his name and identity before reaching the new world. The very generous or romantic might hope that he became sheriff of some small town in one of those square shaped states in the middle, or even staked a claim in the California gold rush of 1849, telling disbelieving miners of how he once knew the Duke of Wellington. Whatever his destiny, he became untraceable.

Compton and the committee now had to save the club. This they did with great dispatch and the help of an appalled but loyal membership. The immediate debt was answered by 40 members who each contributed £100 in return for life membership. An annual shortfall of £320 still needed paying: Compton asked all members to make a voluntary payment of £8. The members rallied. By Christmas

160 members had paid, by the end of January, 1843, 260 had made the contribution and by May, 393, around a third of the membership, had donated.

In the main, members were perfectly tolerant of these unexpected impositions, determined to preserve their club from the bad ending of one man's fickle adventures. Even those who had proffered their resignations before the disaster withdrew and maintained their subscriptions. Naturally, there were complainers: in March, 1843, the committee received a letter from Captain St Leger stating that, having given his £8 towards "the disgraceful losses of the club", he would never enter it again. As a mass, however, the members eagerly demonstrated their determination to preserve their club.

Further economies were still required. Compton was elected chairman for a second year, a rare thing in those days, and started making cuts. The steward had his salary reduced by a third, from £150 to £100; the waiters all lost £2 per year; the steward's room boy lost half his clothing allowance; the staff pew at St George's Church was abandoned; and the members were forced to forego their customary free snuff. It was enough: the club was saved.

Of course, with Cornish learning how to use a six-shooter or pan the icy streams of Yosemite, the club needed a new secretary. Whereas he had failed to survive on £300 per year, the committee now offered the post at £200, inviting disaster and the services of Mr Abrahams, appointed on the 14th of November 1842. The committee, now very wary of secretaries as a breed, clearly offered him much criticism. He wrote to Compton on the 3rd of April, 1843:

Sir,
This expression of disapprobation I have heard with great surprise and deep concern. I have attended 12 hours daily since my appointment to the office, with one or two exceptions only... and I can conscientiously aver that I could not have done more if my life had depended on the result. Yes, instead of going to church I have devoted each Sunday to the interests of the club...

Compton still sacked Abrahams, although the poor man was allowed three months salary in lieu.

A more permanent appointment was given to an old club servant, Edward Sturt, who had previously held the mediaeval sounding title of clerk to the kitchen. He was paid even less: £150 per year, but stuck with the secretary's job until his death eight years later. He had a long illness and when he died in 1851 his brother wrote to the committee thanking the club for its kindness in nursing him. Kindness soon ended: Sturt's family was "reduced to near destitution" but the members could give the widow only £61 and three shillings, a small sum even then.

Compton and Sturt between them brought the Cornish crisis to a happy ending. With the blessed luck of survivors, the club recruited 100 new members in the early months of 1843. The money was well used: 27 of the members who had subscribed to the emergency fund in return for life membership got their money back along with the expectation that they would now continue to pay their annual subscriptions like anybody else; and the club's bank loan was reduced from over £20,000 to £17,800 in May, 1845. The drastic cuts to club salaries were replaced: the steward got back £25 of his lost £50 in 1844 and others who had lost gradually redeemed their losses during the mid-forties.

The members and their representatives on the successive committees had trusted

Cornish for 14 years. They learned a lesson. Secretaries would now be known friends of the club before appointment; known for their dedication to the club and known well by at least a number of members. More importantly, it was clear that change was needed. Revenue had to be generated and not only the rules but the very fabric of the club would have to change.

NO DOUBT the members of the Oriental Club were hospitable men at home but in their London mansion they huddled behind barred gates until the committee recognised that guests too would need victualling and provide revenue. The issue of strangers and their entertainment did not occur to the club until after the Cornish debacle and the realisation that, however exclusive, the Oriental could not afford to turn down business.

The campaign of the generous hosts was long and arduous, starting back in 1840 when A J Anstruther attempted to fill the petition necessary to call an extraordinary general meeting "to determine a proposition for admitting strangers to dine at the club under certain conditions." He failed. The club continued its harsh policy, reprimanding Major Willock for bringing in his young nephew in November, 1841. He reasonably argued that other clubs overlooked the entertainment of close relations and understandably complained of the "exclusive mode adopted by the Oriental Club."

Eventually the better hosts in the club made progress. After wide-spread rumblings the committee received a note of "a very generally expressed desire ...that some regulation should be made for the admission of visitors to dine at the clubhouse." In April, 1842, six months before Compton received the dreadful letter from the secretary, the committee acquiesced to a ballot paper to be left on the drawing room table. The column in favour of welcoming visitors was filled; the column against was entirely blank.

Clearly the members loved the idea of using the club as a place to look after their friends. Equally clearly the committee hated the idea of change. That august body prevaricated, to put it kindly, lied, to put it accurately. The committee stated, on no evidence, ignoring the drawing room ballot, that there was "a strong feeling in the club hostile to the admission of strangers." Committees commissioned to design a horse will always submit drawings of a camel; thus, in 1842, the committee elected to represent the wishes and requirements of the membership employed diversionary tactics in order to subvert those obvious wishes and requirements.

At the annual general meeting in May, the same meeting which was wise enough to elect Compton to the chair, the committee raised the question of sick officers on furlough. This most scarlet of kippers was supported by the fact that, of 165 officers home on sick leave from India the previous year only two had joined the club. The committee proposed that "Officers of Her Majesty and the Honourable East India Company's service visiting England on sick leave from the Government be admissible to the club as visitors for the period of their leave on payment of an annual subscription of £8." This perfectly reasonable motion was carried by 44 votes to 18. Sir Thomas Colebrooke put an equally reasonable motion to this meeting of 62 of the committee's favourite members: the humble suggestion that members be allowed to offer dinner to one guest daily. He was defeated.

Next year's annual general meeting, in May, 1843, found a committee and membership more open to change in a club that had only just survived the defection of its secretary with its funds. Colebrooke persuaded the meeting to allow guests to house dinners, although their meal would cost their hosts 15 shillings rather than the 12 paid by members. A small victory; it provoked the dreadful revenge of the committee men.

Guests were not to find any great comfort at the Oriental. The committee of the 24th of July, 1843, a few months after Colebrooke's triumph and after the departure of Compton, resolved

> ...that the small room adjoining the entrance hall, at present used for urinary purposes, be converted into a waiting room for strangers.

Guests would be allowed into the other precincts of the club but not until their hosts came to rescue them from gleaming porcelain and fearful plumbing. The committee had connived at their convenience.

The annual general meeting of 1843 debated a motion:

> That members of the club who may have with them in London temporarily, sons or nephews or other young gentlemen (being minors) to whom they may stand in the place of parents, shall be allowed to bring them to breakfast, lunch or dinner.

This gentle idea was politely heard and swiftly dismissed.

It took only a month before the 40 signatures required for an extraordinary general meeting were assembled. Colebrooke's original proposition was ratified and each member could now invite one or more guests daily. Ever gracious in defeat, the committee insisted that they would not be allowed in the coffee room.

A strangers' dining room and ante-room were created out of a space which had previously been for sporting rather than urinary purposes. The billiard room had to go to accommodate six tables, each of which would immediately costs its occupants one shilling and two pennies, with another shilling for each bottle of wine. It was made clear that guests were unwelcome elsewhere.

Six years later, in 1850, the club overcame its painful shyness and guests were made to feel that they were more welcomed that suffered. At long last the business sense of the committee would coincide with the natural hospitality of the members.

IN ITS late teens, in the mid-1840s, the Oriental Club had begun to outgrow its surroundings. Wyatt's dark, low building could no longer hold a thriving membership and the addition of guests simply strained further the seams of 18, Hanover Square. In 1844 the club had 542 members; 597 the next year. Since members in the east did not always know of their status, and some still thought they knew but were unrecognised at the club, the full membership cannot be calculated now any more than it could be by the committees of the time. Some tanned servants of the east were still returning to be disappointed at the door; some confused servants of the east were still finding that annual deduction from their bank accounts slightly mysterious.

By 1847 the members rebelled: 633 was too high a number for the club facilities. On the 1st of November the committee received a note with many signatures insisting that that day's ballot for new members be cancelled because:

> ...there are already eighty or ninety members more than the printed rules of the club admit and neither the establishment nor the premises are calculated to accommodate such an extraordinary excess without manifest inconvenience to the other members of the club.

This note suggests not only that the members had forgotten that the club had overreached the membership of the original prospectus very soon after its foundation, but also that, by the late 1840s, it was popular and thriving with a demand far outstripping supply.

There was nothing for it but physical expansion. On Hanover Square the potential for imperial conquest was limited so the club would have to go closer to the heavens. A provision of £2,387 was made for an extension. The most energetic advocates of expansion were the billiard players and the smokers, 30 of whom wrote to the committee on the 28th of June, 1852:

> The lack of a good smoking divan and smoking billiard room in the club is a source of great inconvenience and discomfort to the members, and very injurious to the interests of the club.

The image of retired gentlemen returned from India sprawled across a silken, gold-tasselled divan, sucking on the bejewelled hoses of a steaming hookah must almost certainly be inaccurate.

The committee moved with admirable speed, inviting four architects to submit plans for expansion. Decimus Burton was chosen.

He was one of the most prominent architects of his age. He was helped by his father, a property speculator, and his father's friend John Nash, but Decimus was quite capable of creating fine buildings on his own. Sir John Summerson, so brutal to the club's original architect Ben Wyatt, has nothing but praise for Burton:

> Before he was 20 he had designed his father's Regent's Park villa, 'The Holme' and when he was 21 Cornwall Terrace was being built from his designs. At 25 he was commissioned to design the two works by which he will always be remembered - the screen and arch at Hyde Park Corner.

The screen and arch, of course, provide a neat connection with the club: they were for the benefit of the glory of the Duke of Wellington.

Burton did not need the Duke's patronage as Wyatt had, and could not have had it since Wellington died in the year of his Oriental commission. Burton had already proved himself a brilliant maker of clubhouses. The stately form of the Athenaeum, which he built between 1827 and 1830, was all the qualification he required. He made plans for two billiard rooms over the drawing room and library on the Hanover Square side, raising the building by one story but shamefully omitting any facility for the divan so devoutly desired.

The builder contracted did not have a name as classical as the architect: his was a biblical appellation; William Cubitt might never have measured planks of gopher wood but he had constructed most of Belgravia.

A few of the original debenture holders, those who had taken up Sir John Malcolm's subscription to pay for the site and building of 18, Hanover Square, suffered the jitters. In February, 1853 they suggested investigations of whether the walls of the clubhouse, their only security, could support the extra weight of Burton's upward extension. The club's solicitor, William Ford of Gray's Inn, was intolerant of such timidity. With all the dignity of his profession he declared that unless there was "a risk of the whole building falling in and becoming a heap of ruins" there could be no justification for spending a further £20 and risking the delay "inseparable from consulting Counsel of eminence." He felt, quite rightly, that no less than the physical collapse of the Oriental Club could justify troubling a barrister.

Work started on the 8th of August, 1853 and was complete within three months; testimony to Cubbit's skill. Counsel was not troubled; the building stood.

Only the card players complained. They had good reason; since 1843 they had been crowded around only three tables in a tiny room on the first floor, the use of which returned a quite generous £42 per year to the club. One keen gambler, Captain MacMullen, resigned because he could not,

> go to the club for a rubber of whist and to meet my friends in a small room where my health was likely to receive serious injury.

When Burton's extension was proposed the card players were promised a room on the new floor. It was never delivered; the expense, claimed the committee, would be too great. The card players grumbled for decades:

> annoyance and discomfort are frequently insufferable... close, confined, unwholesome atmosphere... small room crowded to suffocation.

The committee were not helpful, never intended to be, and the card players had no ace to turn.

Perverse fortune scowled on the expanded Oriental Club. Subscriptions and receipts fell off once more in the early 1850s. A compulsory charge of £2 had to made on all members to make up the unexpected costs of the building work and help fill the gap left by shrivelled revenues. Once again, the club was in financial difficulty. Now the answer seemed to lie in amalgamation.

THE FALL off in revenue suffered by the Oriental Club in the early 1850s had been exacerbated by the opening of a rival on the 1st of January, 1850. The East India United Service Club had been founded at a meeting in the British Hotel, on Cockspur Street, in February, 1849. As its first members entered its doors eleven months later it quickly siphoned off those returning from India who might have joined the

Oriental. It origins are obscure but the *East India Army Magazine* of July 1853 reports that:

> The proposal for starting an 'Indian Service' club in the great metropolis originated at the Cape, amongst the 'Hindus', as the Indians on leave are there irreverently termed...

The writer had at least overcome the tiresome old habit of spelling the acolytes of that great faith with two 'o's, and the word 'Indians' referred to those British who had served in the sub-continent; but his story is highly unlikely. Few people changing ships at the Cape of Good Hope would have been ignorant of the hospitality available at the Oriental Club. If there was a need for a new club it was caused by the Oriental's strict attitude to those returning on furlough. When the committee had sought to distract members from the issue of guests it had proposed temporary membership for those home on sick leave, and thought that a great liberalism. Healthy officers returning to "the great metropolis" were naturally welcome to join the Oriental, but they would be expected to pay the full entrance fee and annual subscriptions when they intended to spend many years back in the east.

The East India Club also attempted to be more of a mess than the Oriental. It was open only to officers of the Company or of the crown, along with some other specifically defined categories. Without ever being explicitly rude, it was not for merchants and administrators. No offensive challenge was ever meant, but from the 1850s the Oriental was much less used by military men: it became the club of business, the *raison d'être* of empire; and governors, the authority that justified empire. The soldiers, the brute strength that powered empire, would now tend to go to the new club's building on St James's Square. The blue and gold officers of the Royal Navy, ever careless of such pedantic distinctions, were just as happy to take a glass in either club.

The opening of the East India Club certainly hurt the Oriental's finances. At no time, however, was there a personal rivalry. The fact that they shared the same constituency, the small proportion of Britons who had survived three month voyages in both directions, meant that they had overlapping memberships and common interests. If proof were needed the second chairman of the East India Club, Malcolm Lewin of the Madras Civil Service, left that office only to become chairman of the Oriental from 1850 to 1853, and again in 1861 and 1864. As a governor, rather than a soldier, perhaps he felt more at home in Hanover Square.

Before the East India Club opened it had sent out 4,000 circulars in Britain, and received only 80 applications for membership. Officers in the east were more productive: 3,000 signed on, though the new club was paid by only a fraction. When the first drink was served it had 133 members in Britain, 521 temporary members on furlough and 2,380 in the east, of which 1,200 subscribed for a second year.

The first move was made very quickly by the East India Club. On the 20th of October, 1851, Malcolm Lewin, in his capacity as chairman of the Oriental, received a letter from the chairman of the East India Club that a meeting on the 13 of October had resolved:

> That a suggestion be made to the committee of the Oriental Club for a union, and that if favourably received, a deputation be proposed to be made by each club to discuss the terms on which the two clubs can unite.

By a bare majority, the Oriental committee appointed three delegates: Colonel Bagnold, Lieutenant-Colonel Taylor and Mr Viveash, all of whom knew of their club's reduced revenue, none of whom were willing to reveal it. The East India Club's representatives came to Hanover Square and after some unrecorded dispute over finance, the negotiations failed.

For the Oriental Club, the expensive extension now seemed all the more important to attract further subscriptions and increase business.

The work of Decimus Burton failed to attract new business and had cost the club dearly. Now it was the turn of the Oriental to approach the East India Club; the modest proposal was sent on the 30th of October, 1854. Whether really uninterested or still smarting from their previous snub, the recipients sent back unacceptable terms:

1. Limitation of the admission of Oriental Club members to classes admissible under East India United Service Club rules.

2. Non-liability of East India United Service Club members for any Oriental Club debts.

3. The bringing into the common stock by the Oriental Club of realized [sic] or available property not less in extent than the sum which their collective donations [entrance fees], at the rate fixed by the East India United Service Club for members entering by ballot, would amount to.

The mis-spelling probably put off the Oriental committee from the start. A further insistence that the Oriental sell up in Hanover Square and its members migrate wholesale to St James's Square, a more desirable part of town, and hand over the sale money, was an added insult. The greatest stumbling block, however, was the first condition: many Oriental members in the east were not admissible to the East India Club, and the Oriental would not abandon them.

Mr Bunbury Taylor was secretary of the East India Club. He suggested that the Oriental put forward its own terms, ignoring the unacceptable first condition. The Oriental committee proposed to negotiate as before with a delegation of three. The East India Club would welcome those three but they must face their own full committee.

This presumption that the Oriental must make its case before a tribunal was an unforgivable slight. Whatever the financial trials of the club, such presumption was intolerable. Besides, the Oriental had just received a better offer.

Chapter IV

Victorians

THE ORIENTAL Club found financial safety and an interesting new membership in 1854. The committee received a letter that allowed a comfortable confidence in the club's dealings with the East India upstarts. No delegation would have to go and beg for terms of amalgamation. The letter arrived on the 1st of December and enquired whether the Oriental would consider admitting "a large body of the Alfred Club." That institution, founded in 1808, had not survived the lean times suffered by all clubs in the early 1850s. A later extraordinary general meeting was told that "the Alfred Club was breaking up." That meant new members, new subscriptions, new business and new life for the Oriental Club; and no need to go to St James's Square.

Unlike the East India Club, the Alfred had absolutely nothing in common with the Oriental. It was full of literary types and the sort of clergymen who had already caused the Oriental sufficient embarrassment at the card table. Nevertheless, the traditional confusion over membership was repeated because, like the Orientals, a large number of Alfreds spent much time in corners of the Earth distant from the West End. That travelling connection must have relaxed many shy, or arrogant introductions in Hanover Square.

Denys Forrest's history of the Oriental Club is almost always a generous work but he is rather cruel to the Alfred, describing it as "a sort of secondary Athenaeum, with a lower IQ." It is possible that all the universities of England, though not Scotland, have a lower collective IQ than the membership of the Athenaeum.

It is also true that the Alfred was not noted for its intellectuals. The club was once dominated by bishops, so much so that one story, almost certainly untrue, tells of a mass resignation of members when they found themselves outnumbered in the drawing room by princes of the church. The Alfred was also full of bankers, a healthy counterweight of Mammon, including three of the great dynasty of La Touche.

Its most important literary member was Lord Byron who, being "mad, bad and dangerous to know," might have appreciated the certain welcome of club membership. He was never much liked by bishops, however; half-incest (he was rather fond of his half-sister Augusta) and whole debauchery were not approved. Byron enjoyed the Alfred Club because "it was a decent resort on a rainy day." During a period of vegetarianism, on the 8th of December, 1811, he wrote to a Mr Hodgeson:

> The Alfred has 354 candidates for six vacancies. The cook has run away and left us liable, which makes our committee very plaintive. Master Brooke, our head serving man, has the gout, and our new cook is none of the best. I speak from report, for what is cookery to a leguminous-eating ascetic? So now you know as much of the matter as I do. Books and quiet are still there, and they may dress their dishes in their own way for me.

In 1811 the Alfred was doing very well if it really had 354 candidates for six vacancies. On the 5th of April, 1823, 12 years later, Byron again mentioned the Alfred, this time in correspondence with the Earl of Blessington:

> Tell Count D'Orsay that some of the names are not quite intelligible, especially of the clubs; he speaks of Watts' - perhaps he is right - but in my time Watier's was the dandy club, of which I was a member. He does not speak of the Alfred, which was the most recherché and most tiresome of any, as I know by being a member of that too.

Bishops can be tiresome and perhaps the Alfred became a little too recherché for them when it introduced a billiard table; the prelates resigned en masse. A more prosaic but more accurate description is in William Fraser's *Disraeli and his Day*, written long after the demise of the Alfred:

> The first club to which I belonged in London was in Albermarle Street, the Alfred, a sort of minor Athenaeum. It was suggested to me by my great-uncle, Mr Henry Holland, who had been at one time Lord Grey's secretary, and member for his father's pocket borough, Okehampton. The club no longer exists. The name by which it was usually known was the 'Half-read' Club.

The Alfred was not the greatest read body of men in the world, nor the best informed. Their worst incident occurred in 1827 when, enjoying a house dinner, the members were very unsympathetic to a late comer, improperly dressed. He did, however, prove to be perfect company, witty, interested in the other members and uncommonly well-informed about the political matters of the day. He charmed his fellows absolutely; so much so that when he made his apologies to leave, to continue his work on some papers at home, other members pressed him for his address so that all could stay in touch. Slightly bewildered, he was happy to tell them where he lived; his house was number 10, Downing Street.

The unrecognised prime minister was George Canning who, after that dinner, first christened the Alfred the 'Half-read' Club.

The details of the merger were simple. The Alfred was desperate: the primates were returning and many members were agreed with Lord Alvanley who "stood it as long as he could and only gave in when the seventeenth bishop was elected." Whether the mass of mitres caused the demise of the Alfred or, as one report suggests, a destructive argument on the subject of smoking, the club needed a rescuer.

The Oriental needed the extra members, but it was not going to confess that fact. Talks started within a day of the Oriental's receipt of the Alfred's letter on the 1st of December, 1854. While the Alfred referred to an 'amalgamation', the Oriental chairman, Joseph Glen, insisted on calling the union an 'admission'. Negotiations were short: it was agreed that the Alfred members would be accepted into the Oriental without ballot or payment of an entrance fee, but that they would pay the £8 annual subscription and the Oriental's recent £2 levy for the work of Decimus Burton. The terms took effect from the 1st of January, 1855, all Alfreds to be welcomed if they subscribed within six months. The Alfred's wanderings caused some confusion as they returned to find their club extinguished but the Oriental, experienced in this sort of confusion and still with some original members untraced, took a very generous view of the prodigals.

Negotiations were so swift that by the 14th of December, 1854, 170 Alfreds had joined the Oriental, by the exhausted club's last general meeting on the 21st of December, 240 more, and by the next April another 272 had joined the Oriental on the generous terms of the merger.

They were trouble, as must be expected of literary men: £18-worth of broken glass and china in March, 1855, was blamed on "the unavoidable confusion attendant on the admission of the Alfred members." Many of the old Alfreds left the Oriental in the years after 1855; some just disappeared, a large minority managed to raise their IQs sufficiently to join the Athenaeum. A couple of hundred stayed on and became sturdy supporters of the Oriental. The last member of the Alfred to survive in the Oriental died in 1899.

Sufficient Alfreds remained that their old club is almost a foster parent to the modern Oriental. The Alfred personality, bookish and a little vague about prime ministers, became part of the culture of Hanover Square. In 1855 the two clubs' histories were as diverse as their futures were shared. The Oriental rejected the harsh courtship of the East India Club and seduced the helpless Alfred Club. Consequently, it lost some of the military flavour it had inherited from the Malcolm generation, and gained some element of urbane, Byronesque sophistication from members who might never have travelled east of Tower Hill.

THE NEWLY installed Alfreds were the beneficiaries of an experienced and effective staff at Hanover Square. The club did not quite have the lavish complement of a grand hotel, in which staff outnumbered guests by two to one, but it did have a large crew ranging from the steward, who acted as a sort of vizier to the secretary's sultan, to six or seven page boys who, from 1868 to the late 1930s, were turned out like little generalissimos in beige uniforms with much gold frogging. In an age before electricity and the combustion engine, every middle class household had an extensive staff. One of the advantages of a club to its members was the availability of servants with an automatic economy of scale; many heroes could share one valet. Even so, six chamber maids in 1870 seemed a little excessive when the club was yet to provide bedrooms.

They were part of a staff of around 50 in the second half of the nineteenth century. Members tended to take a benevolent, patriarchal care of the servants. The club was, after all, a small community; of the 50, only six lived off the premises, each drawing an annual £5 "lodging-out" allowance. For members, the Oriental was a convenient dinner and a drink with friends, for the staff it was home.

Only in 1865 did the committee organise a coherent and regular pay scale. The sums seem to be Dickensianly mean although they were exclusive of board and lodgings and were no smaller than could be expected as remuneration for domestic service at other clubs or in private homes. A one pound increase was provided for each year in service, usually only up to the fifth year; again, this seems mean but the late nineteenth century in Western Europe hardly felt the breath of inflation. The crucial posts were:

> Head waiter, strangers' room (Collins); £55-60.
> Carver (Woodcock); £30-£35.
> Butler (Carpenter); £28-£35.
> Night porter, (Howard); £25-£30.
> House porter (Green); £25-£35.
> Coffee room waiters; £25-£30.
> Steward's room boy: £6.

Six pounds is, indeed, a pittance for the year, but he was not expected to remain a boy for ever. Promotion was often possible within the club. Perhaps 10 per cent of the staff served their whole working lives at the Oriental.

Terms of employment were straight out of *Hard Times*. Nobody could expect a pension but provision was made in exceptional circumstances. In 1842 J Weaver, a lampman, was badly burned in a gas explosion and granted 10 shillings per week until he could work again. After five years the committee felt that "he ought e'er this to have found other service" and reduced his payments to 5 shillings per week for one more year, together with an outfit allowance. Weaver protested that his circumstances were special: his injury was caused by "a very imprudent order of the late secretary" (Forrest speculates: 'take a candle and look for the leak'), and, supported by the club doctor, he demonstrated the "utter uselessness of his hands." The full payment was restored until his death 29 years later in the London Hospital, at which the club paid his daughter £3 for a funeral.

By 1877 pensions were more common, though entirely at the committee's discretion. Another lampman was awarded 12 shillings per week after working for the club in that dangerous profession for 48 years and two months. Still, service to the club had to be measured in fractions of a century rather than mere number of years before the committee would relent. Samuel Smith retired after 30 years as coffee room superintendent in 1859, with 50 guineas per year, although a motion to make it his full salary of £60 was defeated. W A Collins, head waiter in the strangers room, enjoyed £50 per year, almost his full salary, when he retired in 1880 after 47 years.

His pension was to cost the club only £100 but another £25 was voted to a widow "left almost destitute." The membership as a whole rejected the committee's meanness at the 1884 annual general meeting: Mary Hewright, head housemaid for almost 30 years, would have her allowance doubled from the proposed five shillings per week.

Such modern provisions as health care were unknown. After 20 years as a housemaid, Anne Adams was forced to retire by rheumatism: the committee recorded only that she "solicited a little assistance towards purchasing furniture for a room." When members of the staff did fall ill they found that dependable support was almost always present. The members, if not the committee, usually managed to find hospital beds for the servants. From 1826 right up to the inception of the National Health Service in 1947 the club insured the staff's health by paying subscriptions to the dispensaries of the parishes of St George (Hanover Square) and St James (Piccadilly), as well as £10, then £20 to keep a regular "medical attendant to the establishment." If the terrors of Victorian medicine seemed inappropriate the club was perfectly happy to prescribe a more tender dose: Richard Cook, coffee room waiter, was granted two bottles of port each week until he felt better.

Almost from the foundation, the club had awarded a Christmas bonus of a pound to every member of the staff, and provided £4 each for a feast which gradually developed into one of the Oriental's great institutions, the servants' ball, welcome to family and friends. Then, in 1861, the billiard room money boxes were broken into, "many other gross irregularities" were committed and the party was over. For over 30 years, the years of bleakest Victorian rectitude, members had no opportunity to thank the loyal friends who forgave their excesses and nursed their hangovers. Finally, in 1893, the committee provided a snivelling £54 to the staff fund. The next year members were invited to contribute independently. They were more appreciative, subscribing £148, 3 shillings and 6 pence in 1894, £160 and 16 shillings the next year and over £197 in 1897. The staff was not quite to enjoy a *fin de siecle* decadence but at least the members would once more provide a Christmas present and throw a feast.

The servants deserved it. From the early times they worked almost flat out, probably 12 hours a day. Since they lived in the club, and normally enjoyed no more than one day off in 14, some must have felt that Hanover Square encompassed the world. The staff and members usually held each other in mutual tolerance. The servants, after all, spent most of their waking hours supplying the members with strong drink and must have excused their regular vacations from rationality. Equally, the staff, often exhausted, often bored, often professionally qualified to use a cork screw, would occasionally find blissful oblivion at the bottom of a bottle.

Three or four day benders were not unusual and almost always forgiven as long as they were not too frequent. Pathetic excuses were gracefully accepted by the secretary and the committee; nobody lost face if even the smallest mitigation could be pleaded. All agreed that the two day disappearance of Charles Willis, bathman, was quite understandable in view of the fact that his beer had been drugged while he was playing skittles.

As often as not, the beer was spiked with alcohol. Members often complained that servants were drunk while on duty. The coffee room waiters were wasted, the cooks were comatose and the hall porters were half pie-eyed. The waiter George Powell bought a couple of mates into the entrance hall to share a dram while the hall porter lay slumbering "apparently drunk." In 1831 the whole staff signed a petition against the steward who habitually pilfered their allowances to spend on liquor.

Before the club had even moved into Hanover Square, on the 21st of May, 1827, the committee heard of a

> ...disgraceful disturbance in the clubhouse at half-past one of the clock on Saturday morning last, occasioned by a quarrel between the butler and five of the waiters ...during which the housekeeper had sent for the watchmen who came into the house to quell the disturbance.

The butler got back to Grosvenor Street at 1.30am, found others boozing in the servants' hall and attacked them. He was a powerful man; his answer to the committee is not recorded but 'you should see the other five' is probably close to the truth. Malcolm and his fellows, magnanimous as always, found him "extremely blameable" and warned him that if ever he struck another servant or even used hard words he would be dismissed, as would the beaten waiters if "another instance arose of their carousing to a late hour."

The club would not always be so tolerant. A committee minute of the 6th of January, 1862, in sterner times, records:

> Harris, the house porter, drunk twice last week. Ordered to be dismissed.

In such a tight community sleeping on the same premises, with fewer beds that servants, bastards were inevitable. Throughout the nineteenth century the minutes occasionally record various maids "sent away". Provision seems never to have been made for mother or child: perhaps some found service elsewhere; doubtless the streets, the workhouse and death were all that lay ahead for others.

Such cruelty was made by the economic attitude of the day rather than any moralistic *hauteur*. When Dr Frere complained that he had found J Boyce and Jas Bridges, both coffee room waiters, "romping with some women" on the front door step of the club the committee found their behaviour perfectly reasonable, if uncomfortable, and wondered at the doctor's naivete.

The clubs health care provisions proved unlucky for one poor girl in particular. The first "medical attendant to the establishment" was a lecherous fellow, as the committee learned on the 12th of December, 1853:

> The under-stillroom maid, Elizabeth Ball, complained that Dr Clerke treated her in a very improper and indecent manner, that he put his legs round her waist, and tried to get her to sit on his knee. He also kissed other members of the female staff.

The committee instructed the club solicitor to issue a summons.

The stillroom was clearly a private place, Elizabeth Ball a beautiful maid and some of the staff libidinous. In October the next year John Davis, a coffee room waiter, assaulted her - "improper behaviour to the under-stillroom maid" - and kept his job only after pleading 26 years service, a wife and five children. The gallant Lieutenant Fowlis threatened to resign from the committee, and the club, because of this leniency, but chose at the last minute to stay and further a more pressing complaint about the Irish stew.

Members gather in the bar.

Members were very rarely unreasonable in their treatment of servants. If they were they usually got what they deserved. One old colonel, late at night, complained that the waiter had cut his cigar inadequately, was told to cut it himself in future, and proceeded to reprimand the author of this advice. The committee quite understood the waiter's reaction and reminded the colonel that complaints about staff should be taken up with themselves, not argued on the spot.

The sometime Bishop of Jamaica, the Right Reverend W G Tozer, an ex-missionary in central Africa, took a more positive attitude to the staff. He attempted to found a library in the servants' hall in 1883, heading a subscription and providing a gas reading light. The subscription was not successful and the hall never became a popular study, but it was a gesture towards universal literacy.

The bishop won much more favour by his kindness to the page boys. The annual outings he organised to the Christmas show at St James's Hall, 'German Reed's Entertainment', became a club fixture.

The page boys' main duty was picking up the members' mail to take to the post. In the age after the penny black, with Anthony Trollope running the Post Office, there were several collections a day. In 1885 they had to be reminded not to go round the club badgering members and telling them to write faster, but to "announce in a loud voice" that they were about to clear the letter boxes 15 minutes before each collection. The final announcement of the day was at 1am, which seemed unreasonable to Mr Allen in June, 1878, who thought it unfair to keep a boy up that late. The duty was taken in turns so the committee thought no harm could be done.

It was a page who prompted the literary talents of Mr Hilton, the secretary, in July, 1870. The boy Varney followed an ancient tradition and slid down the banister of the main staircase, which was almost designed for the purpose. He miscalculated and landed on the couch below, sustaining injuries treated at the Middlesex Hospital. The secretary minuted the accident:

He fell on the ottoman at the bottoman.

THE CAREER of an Oriental Club servant is well illustrated by the affair of Trelawney's hat and the subsequent life of James Dawes, drawing room waiter. In 1831, the year of Dawes' first employment, the committee suffered "mortification" at the amount of stationery and newspapers being stolen by members. On the 7th of November Dawes reported to the committee that writing paper had disappeared on the first, second and fifth, always when Captain Jonathan Trelawney was left alone with the precious materials. Eager to impress, the young waiter set a trap. He and another waiter, Samuel Scott, moved the enormous globe in the card room to the door into the library and hid behind it while they peeped through the keyhole. After a while they saw the captain enter the library, look about for witnesses, grab a sheaf of writing paper and conceal it in his hat.

The sly detectives reported to the committee on the 9th; the captain was confronted with his calumny. He spluttered his innocence, claimed that he had in fact taken two papers from his hat, *The National Omnibus* and *Paris in London,* and donated them to the club. Besides, he pleaded, the staff hated him because he had been heard to say that one waiter, "should never have been promoted from the knife-board."

This called for an extraordinary general meeting, a Cataline trial of the pilfering of papers, chaired by John Malcolm, now back from Bombay. Trelawney found defenders in Colonels Baker, Becher and Tod, who claimed that evidence gathered by espionage was inadmissible and that the spies should be dismissed. Dawes and Scott gave the only corroboration to the story of the other so that Mr Bracken, a brilliant cross-examiner, menacingly remarked that he could not understand how two people could look through the same keyhole at the same time. Scott's written deposition was shaky:

> I sees Captain Trelawney walk in from the reading room and take the paper ...then I takes my head from the keyhole and lets Dawes see ...then I looks againe [sic], then lets James Dawes look againe.

The meeting acquitted Trelawney by 69 votes to nine. He resigned nevertheless, complaining of...

> a system of obtaining evidence which strikes at the root of all morality and social system.

No action was taken against the waiters. Within 18 months Dawes received a pay rise to £25, "his conduct having met the approbation of the committee." Further rises came in 1834 and 1837, he survived an accusation of theft of three sovereigns in 1839 and, four years later, was promoted to clerk of the kitchen when Mr Sturt stepped into Tom Cornish's disgraced shoes as secretary. This was a little above his ability so he reverted to the drawing room within a few months, maintaining his salary of £45 and £5 clothing allowance.

In April 1853 Dawes successfully asked the committee for a raise to £52 and ten shillings after 22 years service, 20 in the drawing room and five as deputy president of the servant's hall, and with...

> pride in saying that he has never been called before the committee for any misbehaviour or neglect of duty.

With his extra money came further responsibility: he would deputise for the steward.

On the 9th of April, 1855: "James Dawes died on Saturday morning." From his early days as a sleuth to the end of his loyal service the committee never knew of his wife and seven children, five of whom were too young to work. It was a familiar story of families rarely seeing servants who lived in the club but utterly dependent on their pay. A subscription was raised but it was not enough. In May the next year the secretary reported that

> ...the widow of James Dawes the drawing room waiter died suddenly and her five children were on the same day removed to the work house.

Captain Gordon was the only committee member in the club when she died. He immediately ordered the steward to pay for her funeral. Jobs were found for some of the children among the members; the oldest daughter was given a clothing allowance so that she could take a position, and £1 a month to look after the youngest infant. The last the committee heard of the Dawes family was from Colonel Bradford, who wanted reimbursement for some medicine he had bought one of the boys who had since left his employment. He was refused.

WAITED ON hand and foot, secure in the future of their club, assimilated with their Alfred brethren and glad to have a home in London, the Orientals could enjoy their environs and tolerate their neighbours. Including the Oriental Club, the north-west corner of Hanover Square housed some of the most interesting, even eccentric residents of the West End, and some of the facades concealed proud, lurid ghosts.

Of course, they would be careful to avert their gaze from the beauty of Mr Alexander's daughters in number 16, now old maids if they were still at home, and look instead at Harewood House on the other side of the road leading north from the square to Oxford Street. This small palace was the home of an eponymous earl, designed by Robert Adam with a bow window and pilasters which might have inspired Wyatt's front to the Oriental. A little to the left, across the access road, was a house once owned by 'Old Jervey', Admiral John Jervis, victor of St. Vincent, from where he took his earldom, once commander and tutor of Nelson. Next was number 16 which became a boarding house when the Alexanders left, providing members with many welcome beds a few steps from the front door of the club. Number 17, the most westerly on the north side of the square had been the home of the great actress, Mrs Jordan, who was the fertile mistress of the Duke of Clarence, later the sailor King William IV. One of their many sons, George Fitzclarence was born in the house and ennobled as the Earl of Munster, thus giving the members a view of three earl's residences in four houses. Munster would live to be wounded in the Peninsula, fight in the Maratha wars, preside over the Royal Asiatic Society and become an original member of the Oriental Club.

The magnificent Baillie propounds a theory that the conservatory was a rehearsal studio for Mrs Jordan, but the thespian had little need to tread the boards by the time she lived there.

Number 17 has other, darker secrets. Just as the Oriental moved into the square it was vacated by the Dashwoods, whose most wicked scion, Sir Francis, had founded the Hellfire Club of West Wycombe Park, and had been reputed to hold delicious, dangerous orgies in his town house.

The Oriental occupied the northernmost house on the west side of the square, separated from the north side by Tenterden Street. The north windows of the club thus looked onto number 3; in which George III had confined the 16-year-old "fair Quakeress" Hannah Lightfoot during his infatuation; in which a bedlam had been housed; and which became the home of William Knighton, apothecary and accoucheur who received it "in acknowledgement of services he rendered in a delicate case" before rising to the office of private secretary to the Prince Regent and dying, a baronet, in Stratford Place.

Number 4, Tenterden Street was a noisy place. The home of Lord Carnarvon in 1793, it attracted the wrath of the anti-papist Gordon rioters who were repulsed by three guardsmen moving from window to window to give the impression of a company. Five years before the Oriental became a neighbour, the house was leased to the Royal Academy of Music, a den of cacophonous brats who allowed members little chance of a siesta.

More tolerant members might have welcomed the musical youth next door. The academy then was not the famous college of the late twentieth century but a school for 10 girls and 10 boys learning their art and inflicting their early mistakes on the district. Edward Seguin, later a famous bass, was a romantic determined to overcome the academy's resistance to the meeting of the girls and the boys. A wall separated the parts of the garden in which the sexes could play: Seguin broke it down with a home-made battering ram. He was also a ring-leader in the persecution of members, once lobbing a lighted candle through the club's skylight. These angelic students took great delight in forming small orchestras to play as badly as possible under the club's windows, something which requires its own peculiar talent, and sweetly asking: "Surely we are allowed to practice?" Musicians are strange.

It was all too much for the steward in 1850. An academy professor came to apologise for a ball thrown through the glass of the billiard room window. The steward could not resist a vigorous and violent defence of Oriental territory and the professor returned bruised and out of tune. The committee patched things up by returning the money offered to pay for the glazing. The steward was secretly applauded throughout the club.

At the far end of Tenterden Street lay Conduit Yard, the lease of which had been bought by the Oriental along with the freehold in Hanover Square. The yard was a mini-Wan Chai, a row of brothels full of women of erotic skill and varied infection. They were comparatively, mercifully quiet.

The whole alley leading off Tenterden Street to the north was illuminated by red lanterns; Shepherds Street, called Derring Street since 1878. Some residents of the square formed The Committee for Preventing Nuisances in the Neighbourhood of Hanover Square in 1844. This committee proved a great nuisance to the Oriental Club. Its solicitors wrote in July that all pimps and madams had agreed to quit or promise good behaviour; the club contributed £10 to their costs. Nine years later Conduit Yard had not paused in its business and solicitors for Lord Carnarvon requested further funds. The club paid £10 on condition that other residents also subscribed. Then the Nuisance Committee again asked for money, within only a few weeks, but the club now had "no funds available." Further money was begged only months later. The club duly paid another £10; commerce continued.

The Oriental was not interested in further efforts to close the cat houses of Conduit Place and Derring Street, they do not reappear in the minutes and they were less trouble than the Royal Academy of Music.

JUST AS the London environment in which the Oriental settled imposed itself into the life of the club and gradually infused its character, the club itself was to become an adornment or, at least, a minor decoration to the capital's great cloth. The Oriental's half-parent, the Alfred, had already been mentioned by Byron as having little rhyme or scan; during the early twentieth century its members would be noted by Lytton Strachey as being a great relief from his more feline friends in Bloomsbury. He found the Oriental so relaxed that once, when he tore his trousers and left them with a tailor, he felt no awkwardness in lunching at the club with a blanket round his waist. In the mid-nineteenth century this fair, rarely vain institution was to be noticed, reduced to paper and caricatured by William Makepeace Thackeray.

Thackeray was well qualified to write about clubmen; he knew their follies and vices all too well and showed them off in *The Fitz-Boodle Papers,* the memoirs of the fat, tobacco-addicted George Savage Fitz-Boodle. This character, as the name suggests, carried on his outrages well south of Hanover Square. Thackeray treated the Oriental more kindly: he was born in Calcutta in 1811 and, having come to England as a child, he relied on the kindness of his extensive family, most men of which were Company officers. His step-father was a Bengal Engineer. Three of his step-uncles were members of the Oriental. One of those, George Carmichael-Smyth, was the panicked commander of the 3rd Light Cavalry in 1857 who ordered the executions at Meerut which helped to provoke the Mutiny.

Gordon Ray wrote in *Thackeray, The Uses of Adversity* that the great social realist "passed his early days as part of a self-contained Anglo-Indian group." Thackeray, like the Oriental, was formed by the mutual understanding of those returned from the east, and their slight isolation from the English society to which they returned.

After all of which he was not qualified to join the club, having never served, governed or traded in the east, and only mentioned it half a dozen times in all his long, tedious oeuvre.

Chapter II of *Vanity Fair* provides the first mention of the club, when Josiah Smedley, Becky Sharp's thwarted marriage prospect, returns from India, rides lonely through the park "and dines at the fashionable taverns (for the Oriental Club was not as yet invented)." The club had immediate immortality.

Many beautiful trees have made the supreme sacrifice for the hundreds of pages it takes before the club's next appearance. Smedley is home again:

> His very first point, of course, was to become a member of the Oriental Club; where he spent the mornings in the company of his brother Indians, where he dined or whence he brought home men to dine.

The Newcomes provides a number of members arriving at one of Colonel Newcome's parties set in the 1820s. Quite accurately for that first generation of members, the friends of Malcolm, Thackeray makes three of them Scots. "Gentlemen from Hanover Square" and "correct East India gentlemen from Hanover Square" surface occasionally to leaven such plot as there is. By chapter XV the colonel needs to leave the country:

> On Thursday he must be up in London, he has important business in London - in fact Tom Hamilton of his regiment comes up for election at the Oriental on that day, and on such an occasion could Thomas Newcome be absent?

He most certainly could not.

Denys Forrest had the sheer determination to become a fan of William Makepeace Thackeray. His words are benevolent:

> *...but my favourite 'Oriental' passage in the whole enormous novel is in chapter XXII and relates to Clive Newcome's historical painting 'The Battle of Assaye':*

So large was this picture that it could only be got out of the great window by means of artifice and coaxing, and its transport caused a shout of triumph among the little boys of Charlotte Street. Will it be believed that the Royal Academicians rejected 'The Battle of Assaye'. The masterpiece was so big that Fitzroy Square could not hold it; and the colonel had thoughts of presenting it to the Oriental Club...

Thoughts shared, one suspects, by more than one actual donor...

Such an enthusiast was Forrest that, like the magnificent Baillie before him, he attempts to discover the real identity of the fictional Colonel Newcome. Quickly dismissing Baillie's theory that Thackeray's step-father is the culprit, Forrest fingers Major General Charles Montauban Carmichael because art and life share a Charterhouse education, the Bengal Army, and the Bath, and both soldiers return to England and election to the club during the winter of 1851-2.

No doubt Thackeray is a titanic writer. He ensures that the Oriental Club will provide a perplexing few moments for every first year English under-graduate and innumerable foot-notes in endless doctoral theses on the impact of Empire on Victorian literature.

BEFORE THE turn of the twentieth century and the old queen's death the Oriental Club needed very little change to its fabric, to its rules and constitution or to its members. Novelty and innovation, when attempted, proved unhappy adventures.

The first was prompted by another sad note from a secretary reduced to emigration, although J H Hilton, appointed in 1851, was not a thief like his predecessor Tom Cornish. In 1871 the committee met to find a note that he was

...shattered in health with long continuous work and adverse circumstances ...Having a very large family I intend to emigrate to California if I can possibly raise the necessary funds, but even by selling up my home and some promised help from a friend, I can only raise £100 or £200.

The committee could take a hint. Mr Hilton was granted a pension of £100 per year. Payments were made until his death in 1880, by which time perhaps he had reached California, and maybe, using his club catering experience, started a humble hotel chain.

Hilton was succeeded by Captain W F Dadson who found that he could endure only two years on the secretary's salary on £350. On his resignation the committee attempted a dangerous innovation.

The offices of secretary and steward were abolished. The club would now have the services of a general manager (£250 per year), a clerk to the committee (£150) and a coffee room clerk (£70). One hundred pounds a year would be saved. The general manager, Mr Lester resigned after seven months. In March 1875 the committee clerk, William Lane, became 'secretary-manager'. A year later the mean scheme was clearly full of "waste and extravagance"; Mr Fry from the Pall Mall Club was appointed as secretary. Seven years later the secretariat had sufficient status to attract 281 applicants for the job, of whom Major C Cecil Clayton was successful. When he left five years later Mr Arthur Stirling took his place and, such were his charms, the committee finally decided to let the secretary dine with the members to "see what was going on." Many objected that the secretary would now spy on them; the fear of being caught, at anything, was ever present.

Far more divisive than the committee's attempts to save a few pounds were the members' attempts to smoke an innocent, satisfying, health-enhancing cigarette. In 1862 Captain Frank Crossman was severely censured for "a distinct and formal refusal to conform to the rule" when he lit up outside the front door, in the pouring rain, waiting for a taxi. Earlier that year the famous Reverend Mr Oldham, the club's all-night gambler, smoked with a friend in the billiard room to the fury of Mr Anderden who stalked around the table for a quarter of an hour mumbling that the club was "the worst managed in London."

Any objection to smoking was, of course, absurd. For one thing, it makes you live longer. Moreover, all those who had lived in the east were addicted to tobacco, like George Savage Fitz-Boodle, because smoking helped to deter insects and foul smells. The club was schizophrenic on the issue. Cigarettes and cigars were on sale in Hanover Square 30,000 at a time direct from China (revolting tobacco), or from William Dent at £8 per thousand. In 1885 a gas jet was installed for the ignition of tobacco on the front steps, the same front steps upon which the club forbade smoking. Decimus Burton's 'smoking divan' of 1853 had proved inadequate. Clearly the only answer was further building so that the pure of lung could avoid the fumigated pariahs. Mr Clifton, architect, was engaged in 1869. His plans embraced:

> ...the entrance hall, a new strangers room, smoking room and billiard room, alterations to the card room and library, and consequent changes to the servant's bedrooms and basement.

All would cost £10,000. The committee gave him a hundred guineas for his plans and looked elsewhere.

Henry Burton, successor to Decimus, had some better ideas. He simply built a new smoking room over the kitchens. With furniture and fittings it cost only £2,663. This new room, which included a mezzanine for ever after known as the 'quarter deck', would prove far more popular than the non-smoking drawing room with its fine view over the square. It was evidently a magnificent chamber. Nevertheless, in an age when smoking was thought healthy, it did represent almost £3,000 spent on the intolerance of those who could not bear the slight perfume of a little smouldering leaf.

Unlit by the comforting stroke of Swan Vestas, the Oriental had relied on gas illumination ever since the move to Hanover Square. As the new century approached, members became aware of a dangerous new element: electricity. Various electricians offered themselves but the club was reluctant to be shocked. Mr Ball, the club's accountant, was willing to convert the old whore-houses on Tenterden street to house a generator. He was turned down. The American Brush Light Company fared no better in 1885. The Medical and Chirurgical Society, at number 20, Hanover Square, offered to share the power from their generator, but the club would not be galvanised into such an arrangement. Finally, in 1892, the Westminster

Electricity Supply Company's 'low tension system' was chosen above stiff competition from the London Electricity Supply Company's 'high tension' rival.

The wiring was completed, the club plunged into darkness for most of November, and the bills for lighting elevated from £52 in 1891 to £64 in 1892. The billiard room wisely maintained gas as an alternative, "according to the temperature."

BEFORE THE end of the century the Oriental Club very gradually relaxed the qualifications for membership. As far back as 1840 attempts had been made to accept "noblemen and gentlemen not connected with the east," but these had been sternly rejected. At an extraordinary general meeting three years later it was agreed to allow the election without ballot of certain important officials: governors-general (including those of unimportant western territories, like Canada); members of the Company Board of Control; and governors of St Helena and of the Cape. Innocent of any lessons to be learned later in the Oriental card room or the Alfred billiard room, the meeting also extended the franchise to a select group of gentlemen in India who served neither Company nor crown: Indian bishops and archdeacons might also be elected without ballot.

With the coming of the Alfred in 1855 the club had no choice but to welcome inscrutable occidentals, slyly shifting the centre of gravity very slightly west.

Only in the 1870s did the club begin to open to non-Alfreds who had not been east. The invasion was led by Perigrine Birch, a solicitor with no eastern connection, who was elected to the committee and successfully proposed his son, his partner and an articled clerk between in 1873 and 1874. When he proposed another clerk the eastern members mounted a solid defence. He was blackballed.

Birch rallied. He and his friends "entered a combination" and blackballed every single candidate at the next election. Candidates faced an open ballot in which one black ball in ten was fatal so the Birch faction needed only a few friendly members to wreak havoc.

The committee retaliated by circulating a leaflet describing the solicitor's disgraceful behaviour. At the subsequent extraordinary general meeting the members narrowly refused to expel him. The meeting did agree that open ballot was far too bloody a field on which to continue the fight. The committee was deputised to elect new members, success being secured by fewer than two black balls in 12 or three in any higher number.

It had been a hard fight for progress and the extension of the club's recruiting ground. Both sides retired hurt. A more enlightened attitude did slowly emerge. By 1884 the club changed its description in *Whittaker's Almanack* from 'Eastern Empire and travellers' to 'social'. It was a prescient act of self-knowledge.

The identity of the Oriental would remain predominantly eastern. Its character could only be made by the character of its members. By the time Victoria died, those members had often been the heroes or villains of Afghanistan, the Sind and Sutlej, the Mutiny and the north-west frontier. However wide the membership would become in the next century, these people provided the Oriental with its personality.

Chapter V

Decline

BY THE turn of the twentieth century the age of small wars was over. Members returning from the east were rarely soldiers now. However, they did maintain an almost military love of traditions. Some felt that the Oriental, founded by Wellington in 1824, was an innovation in itself. The club was still younger than some of its members.

The most ancient was James Macauley who joined in 1887, at the age of 87, and died in 1901, a year into his second century. One member, Francis Mathewson joined the club in 1900 and made some notes in 1930 of conversations with his colleagues which record that, as a newcomer he sat next to Macauley in the coffee room and was asked :

"I gather, sir, from what your friends said in welcome, that you have come from Calcutta? I wonder if it has much changed since I left?"

"If you will tell me, sir, when you left India, I could reply to your question."

"Let me see, it was in May, 1834... "

The magnificent Baillie clearly knew him well. He describes a slim man with long hair and beard, only slightly grey, and proud of reading *The Times* without glasses on his hundredth birthday; he needed them most of his life but his eyesight improved during his nineties...

His breathing was laborious, and the exertion of mounting the staircase to the smoking room was painful to himself and to those who witnessed it; for he still smoked after he was a hundred years old, was fond of his champagne, and was a chivalrous squire of ladies. We always supposed him to be unmarried, but it is stated that after his death a wife appeared, from whom he had been separated for 50 years.

Macauley died across the road from the Oriental in his chambers at 3, Tenterden Street on the 11th of March, 1901. Fourteen years previously he had asked unsuccessfully for a reduced fee on the grounds that he would probably not have many years' use of the club. The committee received his final complaint about the champagne a day after his death.

He was the most extreme example of the gerontocracy governing the club at the turn of the century. So many members, a majority, were very, very old. Mathewson's 1930 notes recall the venerable atmosphere:

Thirty years ago a young, or even middle-aged member was a rarity. A recently joined member was being shown over. Apparently the scene recalled one of those enclosures in Bengal in which the kindly Jain (who may not kill) interns those domestic animals which are past work. The new member, to the horror of his sponsor, ejaculated, 'Good gad, it's a *pinjrapole!*'

With their advancing years the members tended to pedantry about the smallest rules and traditions of the club, and the pedants were revolting. In 1906 a lady called for the discretely minuted Mr E N. When no servant greeted her at the door she walked into the hall where a page asked her to go to the ladies' entrance 'in a most rude manner'. There she was kept waiting for an intolerable five minutes. Mr E N's complaints were many and frequent:

The secretary told me in effect that he could not be responsible for the manners of the club servants, but as he is a paid employee of the club it is surely his duty to ensure that the club is not inflicted with ill-mannered servants. I submit that the page-boy who insulted my visitor should be instantly dismissed, otherwise I shall resign.

The club was inflicted with ill-mannered members. When the committee told him that the boy had been sufficiently chastised Mr E N ranted in a way that would have seemed as absurd a hundred years before he wrote as a hundred years after:

I regret that the committee should condone such an offence - particularly when a lady was the victim - but their decision is merely another instance of the spirit which has caused the Oriental to sink from its position as a great club to one where lower-middle class merchants, business managers and Jews are put up by members with whom they have business transactions and because they are 'good' for the entrance fee and subscription.

Somebody had to go. Tolerant of everything except intolerance, the committee invoked the ancient catch-all rule against "disturbing the harmony and good order of the club." They delicately told Mr E N where he could find his aristocratic, genteel, gentile men of leisure and expelled him.

While such ruthless purging of the wilfully jurassic could make a more relaxed and cheerful atmosphere it could not provide an elixir of youth. Dinosaurs still roamed the plains of the smoking room and the coffee room was the realm of whiskered woolly mammoths. New, younger members were required if only to amuse the ancient beasts and vary their diet of Mutiny reminiscence and north-west frontier exaggeration. One story of the behemoths survives, although it is probably repeated in every London club: a couple of doddering gentlemen passed the ticker-tape machine in 1914 as it printed SARAJEVO: ARCHDUKE FERDINAND ASSASSINATED - "Bloody typical," one exclaimed, "not an English horse in the first four."

Alert vitality did not throb in the veins of the Oriental during the early years of the twentieth century. London's philosopher-cabbies called it the 'Orizontal'.

Action was taken to rejuvenate an archaic corner of Hanover Square. When Mr Buckle resigned in February, 1905, he did so on the grounds that there were "No bedrooms, no cards played, no country membership." He should have taken more notice of secretarial information: two months previously the committee had decided that bedrooms should be available and poor old Ben Wyatt's creation would once more suffer the indignity of reconstruction. The building had never been beautiful but it would now be more scar tissue than soft visage.

Mr T H Watson was appointed club architect and, on the 10th of March, 1905, he circulated his plans to put two floors on top of the floor previously added by Decimus Burton. All three top floors would provide accommodation. It would not, however, be dedicated to members sleeping overnight when the last train home seemed an impossible challenge. Eight sets of chambers would be let permanently, two at £250, two at £225 and four at £200. Ten bedrooms would also be permanently let at £100 each. Temporary residents would have to hope for one of ten further bedrooms costing them six shillings per night. After 80 years, members of the Oriental Club finally enjoyed the inalienable freedom simply to crawl upstairs.

The work took place during one of the club's momentary periods of prosperity and cost £18,000 for the building plus £3,300 for fittings and furniture. The expense of running the new accommodation was hoped to be £1,970 against £2,650 extra income producing a profit of £680 per year. The sky-scraping edifice would pay for itself after 27 years and the members would have available a new and much valued facility.

Financially, the new rooms made some sense but the domination of permanent residents could not fuel the drive for rejuvenation. The apartments soon attracted the usual, very old members. This was just kindness by the committee. Numbers 2 and 3, Tenterden Street had provided 16 rooms, all occupied by members; James Macauley had died in his home at number 3. These chambers were now to be closed down, putting some of the club's most loyal members on the street. The Oriental would gladly house them.

The temporary rooms were a complete success. They allowed the club to fulfil its original purpose with far greater convenience and hospitality than ever before. Available for periods of up to two weeks, more if not then needed by another member, they allowed those returning from the east a comfortable home in London, a place to live while families in the country prepared to welcome the prodigals, a place to escape the welcome of families in the country and the luxury of a house in town, close to the commercial, political and cultural heart of the empire. Some of the permanent apartments could be hired for periods as short as three months; coincidentally, the length of a usual long leave from India. For six shillings per night the Oriental now provided a true home for "persons connected with the British Empire in the east."

At the extraordinary general meeting held to confirm the decision to build some members rightly questioned the benefit of permanent rooms. The situation of the imminently homeless ones of Tenterden Street was quickly explained and accepted. More salacious objections were soon dismissed; after all, there were perfectly good brothels just a short walk away. Nevertheless, the chairman, Mr G P Field, saw fit to warn members present that...

It might lead to scandal - a man might take upstairs his sister or his aunt, so-called...

The new floors were an important and necessary innovation but alone they could not provide more youthful company for the dinosaurs, as the dinosaurs well knew. Further evolution was required, as proved by a chairman who introduced his mistress as an aunt. Gambling on cards, an old staple of clubland, the reason for the existence of the very oldest clubs and cause of such controversy in the Oriental, was to be reintroduced to the club. After Decimus Burton's extension of 1871 the card players had enjoyed quite comfortable premises. As the club had earned increasing amounts for private dinner parties their salon had been required as a secluded dining room. Inexplicably, successive committees had often been enemies of cards. On the 2nd of October, 1900, the whole committee had met especially to solve the moral problems of

...card playing on a Sunday, jam-puffs in the smoking room and the coffee room being used after one am.

That year the green baize was banished with the graceless advice that "cards can be played in the smoking room." The minutes make no further record of jam-puffs. During the heady days of the 1905 reforms the reformers secured a small victory. Before electronic amusements, gambling was an important diversion to those with rubies, a desperate hope to those with debt, a crucial attraction to a club. Complacency conceded slightly to reality: one room was made available to those who chose to play a hand. It was room number 22, a bedroom with a table.

The bedrooms enabled the club to entertain more fully its members living outside the reaches of London's system of public transport, anywhere between Maida Vale and Mandalay. Beyond that, the rejuvenation failed. The great reptiles still stalked Hanover Square but they would soon be extinct; the membership was old and mortal, and the club could never outlive its dying members.

BY THE time the first world war ended some in the club were just realising that Britain had fought again in Europe and, by gad, it was not against the bally old French this time. Modernisation now occurred at the Oriental.

The first step was a symbol, a pseudo-heraldic emblem for the club. Back in the 1830s the secretary, that thieving traitor Cornish, had made orders for snuff boxes with "the club badge." Such badge is unrecorded. By July, 1864, orders were made for "introducing the elephant onto the d'oyleys" for three shillings and six pence per dozen. Only three years later Mr D I Money complained that the beast represented was "the incorrect figure of the elephant." Clearly the wise old pachyderm was by then sufficiently well associated with the club to attract the pedants.

The animals are available in two models; the big-eared belligerents from Africa, and the smaller-eared, cleverer, sportier model from Asia. The Oriental Club was interested in the Asians for obvious historical reasons but also because elephants were friends to men in India for millennia before the British landed there. Most members still had spent time in the east and it takes a cold heart not to look an elephant in the eye without some murmured greeting. The matter of club symbolism was forever sealed when, in March, 1904, Mr Tarbett Fleming offered the club its bronze beast.

The brazen creature has stood in the entrance halls of the club's homes ever since. She - a quick examination confirms the sex - has attracted absurd stories. Her trunk has been rubbed for luck by all new members and gullible guests to the point that the shine on her nose is more than a girl need tolerate. Most unfairly, she has even been accused of being a stuffed real baby elephant, no sculpture but a creation of deadly taxidermy. In 1946, 31 years after she first entered the club, an expert member, Mr J C 'Elephant Bill' Williams, assessed her to be the model of an elephant 45 years old; a nymph of distant memory for many in the Oriental. Forrest prosaically reports that she had been found on a scrap heap. If so, Fleming was the saviour of a work of art and of the gentle-faced greeting of all the club's visitors since.

So identified with the elephant was the club that as far back as 1885 the committee attempted to register the name Elephant London as a telegraphic address, at the cost of a guinea. The post office did not like it. Other names were mooted: Oriental and Tiger were also rejected. After confused negotiation the Post Office offered Cobra. The hooded serpent served for ten years before the Post Office insisted that Care of Cobra must replace it because, after a decade, it was noticed that all the club's incoming foreign telegrams had been sent to the Cobra Company in the City.

Cobra was kept for inland telegrams but contact with the rest of the world was confused until 1903 when the Post Office suggested Clubcone. The committee preferred not, nor would the Post Office accept a return to the old elephantine theme with Hathi. Finally, in 1905, the committee and the couriers settled on Ganpati, an excellent name for the Hindu elephant festival and, more than 90 years later, the club consortium's racehorse.

The elephant motif confirmed, the club turned to the question of a trunk line. During the first decade of the twentieth century the club finally mastered the chief innovation in nineteenth century communications. Members drew breath, summoned up courage and squarely faced the terrifying technology of the new age. By a bare majority the committee, in May, 1900, voted to install a telephone. It was a controversial decision and remained "under consideration" for two years. In March, 1902, it was resolved that the club should apply for a number on the Mayfair exchange, at the cost of £17 per year and a 12 month wait for the installation of a telephone "close to the entrance door."

Such an intrusion could be allowed no further; in December, 1912, the committee vetoed a proposal that there might be "a second telephonic instrument."

LIKE EVERY every other household in Europe, the club suffered by the inevitable, uncontrollable fatality of the First World War. Those few members young enough found death in Flanders, the majority of old men found useful work at home. After the war Mr David Horn wrote to the committee explaining that he had been chairman four times between 1910 and 1917 only because he was "one of the few idle men in the club."

Patriotism, diluted by a little concern about the war's reduction in business, prompted a recruitment campaign. Kitchener's pointing finger found the sons of all members serving in the forces and offered them honourable membership and use of the clubhouse for the duration. Muddy subalterns responded. During late 1914 and early 1915 ,130 sons of members joined the club. Not all survived but the average age of the membership was reduced by a good quarter of a century. Word spread among military youth so that by 1920 old Afghan and Bengal hands could expect to buy sympathetic drinks for the young veterans of Passchendaele and Jutland. There were few field marshals in Hanover Square but a baton had been handed over. By gruesome irony, the war of young male genocide provided the club with the young members it needed to survive.

Most members in 1914 were too old to fight, many had already fought overseas for much of their lives. The servants, however, were qualified to go to war.

So the staff of the Oriental were encouraged to endure the horror of the trenches and all that miserable poetry. The first committee meeting of the war was held on the 25th of August, 1914, when chairman Horn complained of "the unsettled state of the country." Mr J M G Swanson suggested that able-bodied members of staff should be urged to enlist by the provision of half pay to those in the forces and allowances for their families. Encouragement was hardly needed. Thirty-four members of staff went to fight. Nine were killed; a death rate proportionally greater than that of the British forces as a whole.

In London the home front was staunchly defended. When a bedroom window was unconcealed during one night in 1917 the club was fined £4 for failing to observe home defence regulations that would be known as the black-out 25 years later. The errant member failed to reimburse until the committee stiffly reminded him that as "as a citizen of London and a member of the club" he had a moral responsibility to draw the curtains and pay the fine. Rationing would hardly frustrate the appetites of hungry members, shielded as they were by the economies of scale open to mass catering. Fuel, however, was scarce. In an average year the Oriental burned 212 scuttles of coal each month in the bedrooms, another 45 barrows in the kitchens and sufficient other boilers and hearths to combust 365 tons per year, a ton a day. The last year of the war was chilly in Hanover Square, as the club was allowed only 229 tons of coal, the deficit sent to fire the engines of mighty battleships.

The club was supportive of the war effort; particularly keen to help war charities. Indians were the obvious object of donations; 100 guineas were handed to the Indian Soldiers' Fund and, continuing the appropriate oriental theme, used playing cards were donated to the Chinese Labour Camp at Folkestone in November, 1917. The Chinese, confused to find themselves gazing on the English Channel, were delighted to be equipped for a whist drive.

Many members of the club would have described themselves as Anglo-Saxons. Few, during this war with Germany, were aware of the geographical status of Saxony. It was a rough moment to have German roots in Britain; the king-emperor changed his name. The Oriental would not have tolerated such equivocation. On the 26th of May, 1915, the committee declared that;

> ...in pursuance of the recommendation of the members present at the annual general meeting of the 11th instant... no person, though naturalised, who is of German, Austrian, Hungarian or Turkish origin should use the club during the continuance of the war, whether as a member or a guest.

George Saxe-Coberge-Gotha would not be welcome in the club while his subjects fought in his name; and the Windsor deception fooled nobody in Hanover Square, thoughtless as they were of their own address. Many with such suspect roots would be utterly loyal, said the committee, but they were to be excluded just in case.

Sir John Hewett, Sir Edward Rosling and Mr William Beaumont were the leaders of the 1915 apartheid movement, citing "the outrages, the scandalous outrages" of the German government. They named ten members and demanded that "we should turn them out and stand the shot." No fire was returned.

Majorities on successive committees during the war clearly found such a policy distasteful. Humanity had to be disguised as muddle. On the 11th of November, 1918, the fighting stopped in Europe; fifteen days later battle was joined in Hanover Square. The committee revealed to an extraordinary general meeting that;

> Whereas in pursuance of instructions from the general meeting of May 11th 1915 the committee have called for and received explanations from those members of the club who are of enemy alien origin, it is hereby resolved that no further action be taken.

The meeting erupted with complaint. Speaker after speaker angrily reminded the committee that the 1915 resolution was not to demand explanations but to expel indiscriminately. Anger was increased by the realisation that nothing had been done against the bad old Bosch until February, 1918. Even then only four of the ten potential fifth columnists had been approached and asked to explain themselves. It was an outrage, possibly a scandalous outrage.

The committee, chaired by Mr Claude Macdonald, had three defences. Firstly, those explanations received made it clear that the members in question should not be kicked out:

> ...became a British subject in 1884 ...never visited Germany in my life ...30 years in Rangoon ...two sons in the trenches [British trenches, presumably] and a third in Charterhouse Officer Training Corps...

The second defence was that the club's solicitor had advised that the rules on membership could not easily be changed, certainly not twisted against a long standing member just because he bore a mildly Teutonic name. The third defence was a real lawyer's equivocation; there had apparently been no resolution in 1915, simply the proposition of a resolution which was never then drafted or voted upon. Sir Edward Rosling, one of the more rabid excluders of 1915, stood up in 1918 to explain:

> I seconded the motion, not that there was any motion before the meeting; but there was a strong feeling that something should be done, and seconded what I believed Mr Beaumont was going to frame afterwards and did not frame.

Again, the meeting went wild. The members present insisted on a new resolution, passed definitively then and there, that;

> No person who, or either of his parents is or was a German or Austrian (whether such person or his parents have been naturalised in Great Britain or not) can be proposed for membership of the club.

The Oriental Club finally managed to reject the hated enemy races two weeks after the end of the war, and even then the horrible Hungarians and terrible Turks seem to have been lost in the drafting. The resolution lasted until 1937, well into the period when Germany herself had an unhappy interest in her citizens' parentage. The chairman, Sir Henry Wheeler, suggested to the annual general meeting that the membership bar "should be expunged." One year before the Munich agreement, he argued that the enmity between the nations had abated, that the club could make its own small contribution to peace on Earth and that most members probably carried a little Germanic blood. Only two members disagreed. Any Germans or Austrians who might now choose to join the Oriental would not be rejected for their race.

The whole episode might suggest that the club was full of ignorant, thoughtless bigots, which it no doubt was. More importantly, though, it was suffering the aches of age. The members were still predominantly very old men. They were too ancient to fight, appalled by the new, slaughterous form of warfare they saw in Europe and frustrated that they could do so little to help the ill-defined cause for which their sons and grandsons were fighting. The club was irrational and malicious towards those with Germanic families, but, perhaps, that was a shocked, traumatised reaction to what its members learned of the trenches.

No similar resolution was passed during the Second World War.

WOMEN WERE trouble in the Oriental Club. Presumably they had provided most members with some joy between the nursery and the boudoir. Many members managed to procreate; some doubtless had loving wives, sweethearts, both. In the club, however, they were not welcome. Lady guests were allowed on sufferance but the atmosphere was designed to replace the mess or the hill station or the board room of a trading house, not the salon. The club was not totally misogynistic but it had a bristled fear of emancipation.

Women might, however, make perfectly acceptable servants, especially when the supply of male staff was restricted by warfare. Chambermaids had always worked at the club but servants in the public rooms were resolutely male. The idea of a woman

Alice in the uniform she designed
for six decades of service.

The elephant welcomes all
visitors to the Oriental Club.

servant was first mooted in committee in November, 1915, and more generally discussed at the next annual general meeting after the members had become used to the club's first, pioneering waitress. Mr Robert Williamson put the motion to keep her:

> I believe that no objection will be raised by any member to being served by a nice tidy girl wearing a clean white apron.

Inevitable objections were raised and soon quelled: the pioneer had already put herself in members' hearts. Several girls had turned down employment, repelled by the fusty atmosphere, but, on the 14th of August, 1916, Mrs Hunt's agency in Marylebone Lane sent a young woman who had just refused work at the Piccadilly Hotel at 18 shillings per week. The club offered her 19 shillings and three pence, she quickly realised that she could manage its members and started work immediately.

Her name was Ellen Elizabeth Moore, daughter of a master builder and a washer woman from Kilburn. From her mother she had learned the secrets of starch and needlework and used those skills to design the uniform she was to wear in the service of the club for almost 65 years; first employed during the ministry of David Lloyd George, last employed during the ministry of James Callaghan. During that aeon she was universally and inexplicably known as Alice.

Alice was not the only woman looking after members during the First World War but she was the only one to stay at the end of hostilities. As her sisters deserted her she grew into the role of senior drawing room waitress. As her half-century extended and she gradually overtook the average age of the membership she developed a maternal care for her charges; usually indulgent of their eccentricities but capable of reprimand.

She also became the matriarch of the Oriental staff. Dickens had given way to Dr Arnold in the club's attitude. As well as squalid accommodation and cheap wages the staff had, since the 1880s, been expected to play sports. Off-games notes were not acceptable.

The magnificent Baillie reports that the Honourable Robert Grimston, an Alfred inheritance, was...

> An impassioned diner, and it was dangerous for even a fellow member to speak to him while engaged upon this rite ...one of the kindest and best-hearted men who ever entered the club doors.

Perhaps, but he also had that strange English cruelty that insists on 22 grown men suffering the tedium and futility of a game that can last for five days before all happily settle on a draw. He established a fund to promote cricket. Matches were enforced on Paddington Recreation Ground until after the First World War when Lord Lilford presented a cup for bowling, a team competed in an Inter-Clubs League and matches were organised between members and staff at the houses of Sir Bertram Hornsby in Sussex and Dr Crouch at Ascot. These torments continued until the merciful intervention of the Luftwaffe.

Servants of the Oriental were offered alternatives to the grinding tyranny of cricket. Jack Parsons, who had become head valet in 1917, reminisced to Forrest that he had played

...football on Paddington Recreation Ground, shot at the Polytechnic, boxed at the Sword Club and swam in the Serpentine.

Forrest asked him where they found the time to be such athletes:

Well, I don't know, sir, but of course we were nearly all living in, and somehow though we worked longer hours, things weren't so tight as they are now...

Things were made a little less tight by the creation of a Provident Fund in 1919, supported by a five per cent subscription from employees' wages and a 50 per cent bonus from the club. At last, the staff had some security, long before similar institutions provided any such service. Contributions and legacies would swell the coffers, often from the most unlikely testators; some mean old curmudgeon who "wouldn't pay for as much as a biscuit with his cup of tea" would die to nobody's great regret and leave a small fortune to the fund.

Such measures helped to create a small cadre of staff who, like some nineteenth century predecessors, spent most of their working lives at the club. Parsons told Forrest of the old wine butler, Cunnington, who worked at the Oriental for 40 years before retiring in 1938, famous for his discipline:

...we boys loved to play tricks on him. When he was out serving, someone would make a noise like a cork being drawn - shloop - and he would come rushing back: "Who opened that bottle?"

Parsons himself was only a little less long at the club than Alice and Alice, of course, was almost immortal.

ALICE WAS to be a symbol, almost an icon of the Oriental Club in the years after the First World War. Before that conflict, though, members were still confounded by others of her sex. Their wives were not quite barricading Hanover Square; simply demanding the right to lunch. Fulfilling a stereotype that must have made the club's conservatives smile triumphantly, the pressure to welcome ladies was caused by shopping.

By the late Edwardian years Hanover Square was perfectly placed for the great emporia of central London. In Bailie's time the Square had gained the chic of couture:

Imagine for a moment ...the visits of fair women in elegant carriages to the fashionable modiste who rules the establishment in front of us.

The 'modiste' was Lady Duff Gordon, known professionally as Lucile, the most fashionable dressmaker outside Paris and resident of number 17, Hanover Square until Sir Francis Dashwood refused to renew the lease, at which she moved to number

23. She sold her flappers' frocks in the rooms once inhabited by Mrs Jordan, William IV's beloved actress, and would come to define sartorial taste in the roaring twenties. The Oriental was also the closest club to Regent and Oxford Streets and within walking distance of Harley Street. It was *de rigeur* to have a fancy doctor as well as a fancy dressmaker. The wives and daughters of the age simply had to have the club for after-noon tea, their husbands and fathers for a post-spending cocktail.

The old rule that women were welcome to a few rooms for limited hours would have to be liberalised. Stirrings had first appeared at the 1903 annual general meeting. With great aplomb, Mr G H M Batten suggested that the rules be changed not for the benefit of women but for the delight of the younger members the club needed to attract. He argued strongly that clubs

> ...are not recruited from old gentlemen. They are recruited from young men, and those young men require to find themselves surrounded by the institutions which they are accustomed to.

Those 'institutions' were, of course, young women and possibly, unthinkably, dancing. Batten then ridiculed the extremist opposition:

> Last year one gentleman seemed to think that if we admitted ladies, we would see nurseries of children sprawling over the floor in the smoking room. But ladies would be confined...

The minutes of annual general meetings were taken down verbatim. They then record "Heavy guffaws." Nevertheless, members voted to allow ladies the right to have lunch between one and two-o-clock, as well as tea between five and seven. Reaction was swift. One unchivalrous member pointed out that the club was

> ...the only place in London where my wife cannot get at me - and am I to lose this boon?

Fears that they might hang around all evening were calmed by Mr Crozier: he was sure that they would clear out about 8.30pm and go to the theatre. The next year Sir George Mackenzie successfully moved that ladies should be excluded only on Thursdays, which days were clear for men-only dinners until 1937.

No suggestion had ever yet been made of female associate membership.

INCOME FROM women and the returning soldier sons of members could not provide the club with financial security nor, as the twenties roared, with a less geriatric atmosphere. Immediately after the Kaiser's war the demobilised armies returning from Europe and the east buttressed numbers; adding to their comrades already in the club. In 1919, 94 candidates were elected, to be joined by 85 more during the following year. The post-war boom encouraged shopping but the warriors and the consumers flattered to deceive.

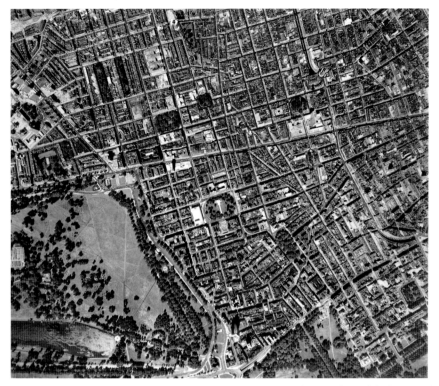

The bombardier's view, with Hanover Square and Stratford Place vulnerable but undamaged.

The library continues the Stratford House tradition of lavish entertainment.

The club was complacent. In 1920 the entrance fee was lifted from 31 guineas to 50 guineas. The annual subscription stayed at the old 1882 rate of nine guineas for existing members but the crucial new candidates were expected to pay 11 guineas in 1919. The old and new rates rose respectively to 11 and 12 guineas in 1921, and 14 and 15 guineas in 1922. An absolute rise in the cost of membership combined with the discrimination against fresh members to cause a fall in recruitment during the early twenties. Not until the worst year of the coming depression, 1931, did the club recognise the need to reduce the entrance fee to the old figure of 31 guineas. The Oriental had already priced itself out of the boom.

One hundred years after Sir John Malcolm had summoned his friends to the Royal Asiatic Society, the club that they had founded was once more in deep financial distress. This time the members and the committees they elected were entirely to blame: no felonious secretary had made the crisis to justify the traditional emergency whip-round.

The Oriental was saved by the foresight of old Duke Arthur. Wellington's insistence that the club own its own building saved it from the fixed burden of rent; all other expenditure could be reduced to the Spartan necessities. Immediate saving was made by abandoning schemes for yet more building. A new club architect, Guy Dawber, had drawn up plans for a total redesign of the monolith left by Wyatt and Burton. The poor, mutilated edifice was saved further indignity by the club's poverty; the necessary £70,000 would never be raised. Dawber was employed on a few lesser projects, rebuilding pantries and designing dividing walls.

Other building works had been planned to mark the club's centenary in 1924. These, costing a mere five or six thousand pounds, suffered the same fate as Dawber's grand design. Such little expenditure as was possible went to a superficial beautification of those rooms open to ladies.

John Malcolm had chatted with Wellington, called two meetings at the Royal Asiatic Society, produced a prospectus, recruited sufficient members and opened a clubhouse. Which event marked the actual foundation; on which day should the centenary be celebrated? The committee of 1924 chose the last, the club's move into its first premises in Lower Grosvenor Street on the 8th of July. The means of celebration were obvious: the Oriental, unsure of its future and very short of money, would have an enormous, decadent, hedonistic party.

A hundred and twenty members paid a very reasonable two guineas each to enjoy the feast. All problems were forgotten as their eyes fell on a sumptuous menu:

	Caviar d'Astrakhan
Pale dry sherry	Tortue Clair au Medere
Graves Superieur	Truite Saumonee a la Neva
Veuve Cliquot (1915)	Escalope de Ris de Veau Clamart
Gruaud la Rose (1915)	Selle d'Agneu Richelieu Taylor
Vintage Port (1904)	Terrine de Foie Gras Lucullus
Fine Champagne	Souffle Glace au Rhum
Courvoisier	Friandises
Liqueurs Various	Cassolettes Orientales Dessert.

The 9th of July, 1924 was probably one of those very quiet, very slow moving days in the Oriental Club. Apart from this bacchanalia the club did little to celebrate other than giving every member of staff a week's bonus pay. The club's first century had been substantially shared by its members, as Forrest delicately suggests:

> A cynic might reflect that the members would have been more impressed with the wonders of being 100 years old if so many of them were not already - but let us move on to other themes...

Methuselah still reigned at the Oriental. Still, secure in its freehold, the club was in no immediate danger. Great changes of the 1920s were not financial but constitutional. Ever since Malcolm's first committee, that parliament of princes and pirates, responsibility for the club's government had wavered between chairmen, secretaries, general committees and house committees and, most often, kitchen cabinets and small juntas of those chosen by allies of the chairman and the secretary. Mr Ebeneezer Henry, elected chairman in 1925, resisted humbug by reducing the general committee from 24 to 12 members. Consequently the general and house committees were similar in size and little was now delegated to the latter. Three years later the two bodies became one. They remained so for six years before the house committee, much streamlined, resurfaced. The chairman of 1934, Mr Charles Findlay, took great pride in reporting that;

> We have, I think for the first time, constituted a permanent house committee of two members and the chairman.

After better information from an anonymous pedant, Findlay withdrew the words "I think for the first time."

These noble new senates dealt with the traditional problems of club life. Little had changed since the days of the Mutiny. A suitably awesome reply was drafted to the enquiries made by Sir J P Hewett's concern about muffins. Learned judgement was handed down to Mr Justice Harrison that

> ...it was decided to say that the servant who had failed to carry out his desires about soup had been admonished.

A stern letter was sent to a member who invited more than two guests upstairs, a particularly heinous crime compounded when one of the guests found it necessary to vomit in the smoking room. Members anxious about the cuisine were gently calmed, as was Sir Ludovic Porter:

> The committee regretted that Sir L P has cause to complain, but assures him that the remnants of the week are not used for service on Sundays.

Occasionally the committee was held responsible for accidents that even its omnipotent powers could not have been expected to prevent. A guest blamed the club directly for a small spillage of gravy on his daughter's dress, adding that the food was "inedible." His letter was quietly passed to the member who had entertained him so shabbily.

It was the long suffering secretaries of the Oriental who had to deal with such unreasonable correspondents. Having learned that the club could not function without secretaries, the committee was grudging in rewarding them. Lieutenant-Colonel Godfrey Bird accepted the job in 1909 at a salary of £250 per year: an astonishing £50 less than Tom Cornish was paid as the first secretary 85 years before in 1824. Bird remained in office for 13 years, retiring in 1922. He had been recalled to the colours during the war and managed successfully to run the club while on active service, responding to complaints about muffins while with his battalion. His salary was substantially higher when he left the club.

Secretaries were so much better appreciated by the 30s that when Major R C B Williams resigned in 1934 the committee could not find a man of sufficient talent to replace him. Money was a consideration, as always, and the cheapest option was chosen. The Oriental would have an unpaid, honorary secretary. This dark shadow fell across one of the club's most regular and loyal members, Sir Alfred Pickford, usually known to members as 'Pickie'. He was an eminent tea importer and famous eccentric: Forrest recalled their first encounter;

> I was confronted by this gigantic monocled figure, attired, unnervingly, in the shirt and shorts of a boy scout.

Pickford worked uncomplainingly as secretary until 1937, and as chairman in 1941. His successor in the secretariat, Colonel A Dallas Smith, like Lieutenant-Colonel Bird, would have his career interrupted by war. Dallas could not fight and control the club as well. The secretariat was again taken by an unpaid member, Mr H A Gardiner, until 1945 when the task was once more handed to the professionals.

The first engagement of the Second World War was fought with the lances of mounted Polish cavalry; the last with an American atomic bomb. The intervening redesign of the world passed the Oriental by with hardly any noticeable effect. Killed and wounded members and staff were very much fewer than in the First World War. Only three servants died on active service. Similar provisions were made for families and salaries as had been made 25 years before. A whip-round for the casualties raised £6,000, almost twice the figure of 1917, compatible with inflation.

Income from receipts and subscriptions fell drastically as a result of the conflict until the committee and senior members organised an aggressive recruitment campaign. After two years during which resignations poured in and the club elected hardly any new members, 60 volunteered or were cajoled into joining in 1941. Fifty of those were attracted by the belated innovation of country membership. Successive committees had been loath to allow those who lived out of town a discount, fearing the immediate drop in income more than the prolonged fall in membership. When numbers became dangerously low in the early years of the war the club was forced to reform. An extraordinary general meeting in December, 1941 failed to get the quorum of 50 but it did provide Chairman Pickie with a boisterous debate. Country members were quietly allowed early the next year, paying only 10 guineas per year if they

...do not live within 100 miles of Oxford Circus or have their regular place of business in London.

Now that those who used the club only rarely were not expected to subsidise the regulars' fees, membership became very much more attractive. The new men in Hanover Square were not numerous, but they replaced the losses and saved the club from a withering death.

As in the earlier conflict, rationing was little hardship. Club catering could accommodate most appetites. The Oriental became a famous meeting place, celebrated in the Peterborough column of *The Daily Telegraph*. On the 10th of April, 1945, the columnist speculated that the club's food was so good and so plentiful because of its situation

...far off the Whitehall lunch route, [so that a meal could be had] without being trampled under foot by that howling mob of starving civil servants.

Bombers were unkind to urban Europe ("Good God no, Group Captain, not the Bremen Bearings factory again tonight!") but the Oriental was blithely untroubled by aerial attack. The Luftwaffe probably saw little tactical advantage to the demoralisation of several elderly gentlemen separated from mobs of howling civil servants. If the Germans would not give Wyatt's bunker a glorious end then the British forces would make the attempt; an anti-aircraft shell landed near the hall porter's desk, but even when he kicked it out into the square it failed to explode.

Number 18 was in greater danger from the carelessness of its own inhabitants. When a fire broke out in the messenger boys' dormitory the embattled London Fire Brigade expressed great pleasure in having to deal with "a genuine fire" for a change.

Like most sailors disciplined to the tyrany of the tides, Admiral Donitz was a man of immaculate timing. On the 8th of May, 1945, he considerately brought the European war to a close on Lunneberg Heath just in time for the annual general meeting of the Oriental Club later that evening. Of course, the membership was such that the army in the east was not forgotten, but the 33 men who attended the meeting managed to generate an atmosphere of tremendous relief and rejoicing.

They did not then know that the storm clouds were just gathering over the Oriental Club.

Chapter VI

Exodus

BY THE end of the Second World war the Oriental Club was still largely inhabited by dinosaurs blissfully ignorant of the imminent risk of extinction. The political separations of India, Pakistan, Burma and Ceylon made little difference to existing members; they merely tightened the bond between the old eastern hands and made the club all the more useful to members from the newly independent nations who had business in London. New members, however, were no longer as likely to be recruited from the British service in the sub-continent. The British had gradually been extinguished in the Indian Civil Service, old Indian army officers were either retired or had their chain of command severed from Whitehall. Trade continued, of course, and various migrations in both directions ensured a thriving Anglo-Indian community in Britain and the Orient, but the club still could not attract a viable infusion of fresh blood.

Small things like the Second World War and Indian independence were much less harmful to the club than the greater forces that had been present since before 1914. Founded by and for men who had fought in the Napoleonic wars and made India dependant, the Oriental was suffering the social, technological and financial condition of the twentieth century.

Anachronism was inevitable because the demands the club was designed to answer were no longer made. Stately barques had taken months to carry the original members to their empire: steam abolished the need for the long leave and a temporary London base. Worse, trains let people make a trip to London and then, at great danger to the Oriental Club, go home the same day. Trains and cars had changed London, fewer people lived in the centre of the metropolis where they could pop over to Hanover Square for a drink and a chat. Potential members were increasingly suburban and eager to return to their own little castles. Any hotel or bar could provide a drink after work but the need for a club as a home from home was disappearing.

David Lloyd George must accept some responsibility. His People's Budget of 1909, all death duties and redistribution, might have fed and sheltered millions but it was never pleasing to have to sell the back acre and let go the second footman. The British bourgeoisie, the Oriental's spine, could no longer take for granted such luxuries as a club. Atlee's government and the great depression had further weakened middle-class disposable wealth. Perhaps because of the separations of the Second World War, perhaps because it was cheaper, perhaps because they liked it, men chose to spend their spare time with their wives and families, maintaining children and households without the aid of servants.

Rarely with eastern connections, suburban, poor and domesticated, the bourgeoisie was not in the mood for joining old-fashioned clubs in the late 40s.

On the 31st of December, 1951, the Oriental Club had only 817 members, many of whom remembered Victoria's funeral. It had a mortgage commitment of £41,250, an overdraft of over £15,300 and a revenue account with a deficit of £3,200 and growing. The committee had received an offer of £177,500 for the Hanover Square site. In 1951, it recommended to an extraordinary general meeting that the offer be accepted and that the club go into liquidation. Like so many of its members, the Oriental was very close to death.

The meeting rejected the proposal. Emergency measures were devised by the new committee under the chairmanship of Mr James Macfarlane; an appeal for donations and loans was set up under the aegis of Mr J K Mite. Nine thousand pounds were given, £40,000 lent interest free. One observer remembered that:

> The members of the club who subscribed to the loan so generously were well aware not only that they would receive no interest, but that if anyone wished to obtain repayment on his loan it would be incumbent on him to arrange either to die or to resign.

A recruitment drive brought in a few more subscriptions. More importantly, the emergency prompted a massive change of policy: wives and daughters of members were offered associate membership, a liberalisation still entirely unthinkable in any of London's other traditional clubs. The same observer was rather cheered by the fact that

> ...for the first time in the history of the Oriental Club a member, walking along the corridor in his dressing gown, to his bath in the morning, ran the awful risk of meeting a lady returning from the same mission, clad in the same dissolute garb.

Rarely seen but always appreciated, the kitchen is the engine room of the club.

For the first time without contravention of the club's rules.

Membership rallied: 612 new members joined before the end of 1952, including 270 lady associates. The mortgage was discharged, the overdraft reduced to £8,500. The revenue account achieved a surplus of £900. The salvation of the club was a remarkable achievement, a demonstration of its members determination that the Oriental should survive. Nevertheless, it was first aid, not the radical transplant that the club needed for a long and healthy future.

Profitable accounts continued for only four years. The building needed massive expenditure, far beyond the club's resources, and, in 1956, the club once more made a loss. Sir Robert Hutchings took the chair in 1957 and hit upon the essence of the plan that might save the club. He investigated the possibility of allowing a property developer to exploit the site of the clubhouse, far more valuable than the building. Any new office block would then provide accommodation for the club at a peppercorn rent. On his leaving office he wrote to Sir Arthur Bruce, who had been chairman in 1954 and was the gleeful observer of ladies' dressing gowns. Bruce agreed to pursue the development potential and resume the chair. He would be chairman for four years, and like another Malcolm in his resurrection of the Oriental Club.

His first task was to rationalise the club's finances. The club had lost £1,000 in 1956, £4,000 in 1957 and was likely to lose £6,000 in 1958. The overdraft had risen by nearly £10,000 in three years to £14,000. The bank put on a limit of £20,000. Brigadier R G W Callaghan, the secretary, had the harsh task of making brutal cuts in the club's expenditure. Staff were fired, prices raised, coal counted. A surplus of a few pounds was achieved in 1958; Callaghan had succeeded in a holding operation.

Meanwhile, Bruce searched for allies; the club needed all the friends its members had. None of the committee had any experience of property development. Their ideas were vague at best; there was some despair. Fortunately their chairman had many and wide connections. In true club style, friends of friends got in touch and the club found an honest broker, a determined dealer, a loyal friend and a saviour over one good lunch. Bruce's old friend Mr V A Grantham, chairman of Chartered Bank, put him in touch with a close associate, Mr Aynsley Bridgland. This man lived to be knighted but as far as the Oriental Club was concerned he might have been canonised.

Bridgland was an unlikely saint. He had sustained wounds at Gallipoli that always marked him and he had what obituarists delicately call a direct manner. Most diabolic: he was a property developer, but in an age before that profession had made its modern Faustian pact. Plantation House, in the City, was his work, as was Bucklerbury House where he was appropriately gentle with the foundations of the temple of Mithras exposed by the building site. At first, simple generosity led him to offer his services, entirely unpaid, to the club. Later, after years of negotiation with financial institutions and landlords, builders and local government, he freely confessed that he regarded the whole process of saving the Oriental as a wonderful game in which he, the shrewdest and most cunning player, took the greatest pleasure. The club quickly learned to trust in his skill and benevolence, and asked him to play with its highest stake, the Hanover Square freehold.

Bruce and Bridgland were both old soldiers, the former bearing a Military Cross, that latter the scars he earned with ANZAC. Both must have admired the foresight and strategic planning brought to their campaign by an old commander-in-chief: the orders had been clear; "buy your own property," the old duke had said.

THE FREEHOLD on number 18, Hanover Square was the Oriental Club's only material value. It was 13,550 square feet of some of the most expensive ground in the world. In 1951 a potential buyer had offered £177,500. Now, in 1958 and 1959, the value would be higher but mysterious unless the property were offered for auction. This, Bridgland wisely advised, would not be the most effective way of exploiting the treasured territory.

Whatever value it had was depleted by three factors. First, not all the ground was freehold: the old stables were encumbered both up and down. Up, the club had those premises only on long lease from the City. Down, the club had sublet it to the London Fencing Club and could not dispose of it freely until the 31st of December, 1969.

Second, London County Council had a couple of restrictions. No new building could be built in Hanover Square with a floor space more than five times the ground area; and any new building could have only 70 per cent of its space devoted to offices, the rest must be used for residential or other purposes much less lucrative in rent.

Third, any buyer of the Hanover Square site would have to pay for demolishing the existing clubhouse; poor old Ben Wyatt had meant well but his work never had much sentimental value.

The precious plot was, however, worth enough to save the club. Bruce, in a later memorandum, recalls considering three possibilities for the future of the Oriental. It could still sell or lease the ground to a development company which would house the club in a new building for a nominal rent. It could amalgamate with another club, many of which were in similar distress, and sell one clubhouse to rebuild on the site of the other. It could sell Hanover Square and find or build a cheaper, more convenient building elsewhere.

Two of Bruce's original plans had inherent problems. An offer had been made to lease the site and provide a couple of floors in a new building for the club, but the lease would have been comparatively short, the remuneration was not generous and the members would have had to wait two years for a new construction. Bruce had shyly wooed other clubs for amalgamation, but he understandably found these courtship's distasteful. As with the ancient overtures of the East India and the Alfred Clubs, the Oriental much preferred to be seducer than seduced.

The third option seemed more attractive. Lord Kelsey wanted to dispose of his 950 year lease on Chandos House off Cavendish Square. It was a beautiful Adam building, a little small for the Oriental but with the possibility of extension for bedrooms behind. It had much in common with the club's eventual home: both were built in the 1770s, both had served as the Hapsburg embassy of the extravagant ambassador Prince Paul Esterhazy in the first half of the nineteenth century.

The committee was filled with hope. Specifically, its members hoped that it could sell Hanover Square for more than it needed to buy Chandos House. Hope sprung temporarily when an unsolicited offer was made for Hanover Square of £300,000. Bridgland set his surveyors and architects to work in designing an office block on the site of the club and making Chandos House comfortable. As plans were drawn up sly, clever Bridgland explained to Bruce and the committee another, more satisfying way to save the Oriental. If certain circumstances were to arise, he suggested, like a player waiting for the wild card, the Oriental Club might have its future guaranteed and emerge as one of the richest and most secure clubs in London.

Sir Ainsley Bridgland might not have been a joy to the eye but his financial intellect was as elegant as art. It was madness, he argued, for the club to sell the Hanover Square site to a third party which would then make it a profitable building. The club, he told the dazzled Bruce, must be its own property developer. It must move to Chandos House and build its own office block for rent in Hanover Square, accepting the risk of finding a tenant. The cost of buying the millennial lease of Chandos House and building on Hanover Square would be, he estimated, around £800,000. This could be financed initially by bank borrowings on the security of the two properties and then by a fixed mortgage redeemable after 34 years. The rent from the Hanover Square site would pay the mortgage with a delightful excess of profit for the club. After the mortgage was redeemed the club would own both the freehold of Hanover Square outright and the 950 year lease on Chandos House. As advisors, Bridgland and Wellington had provided the wisdom to preserve the Oriental and give it great wealth.

Brigand's plan had three requirements. It needed willing financiers of the bank loan and mortgage on the two properties; it needed a tenant for the office block to be built on the Hanover Square site; and it needed the new home of the club, preferably Chandos House, to be quickly available at the right price. This was the tripod of Brigand's suggested deal: finance, a Hanover Square tenant and a new home for the club.

One of the legs of the tripod soon buckled. Bruce and Kemsley, vendor of Chandos House, had several very agreeable lunches at which Bruce revealed that he had been advised the property was worth only £125,000 and Kemsley revealed that he would not sell for less than £180,000 pounds. It was an impasse. Talks came to an end in July, 1959. Kemsley had received a good offer from Roy Thomson, proprietor of *The Sunday Times,* and would eventually sell, to their mutual satisfaction, to the Royal Society of Medicine.

Bruce now had a brilliant strategy at his disposal, but not the conditions to employ it. The club was offered £350,000 for Hanover Square, again unsolicited, again cheering to the committee, but without all three strands of Bridgland's master plan the chairman could only note the offer and comment that the future of the club was still under consideration. Brigadier Callaghan, the secretary, maintained his desperate fight to hold down the club's expenditure for another nine months before, in March, 1960, the third, elusive condition of the Bridgland plan became possible.

Birfield Ltd put on the market a beautiful building that they had been wasting as offices. It was Stratford House.

ARCHITECTS AND surveyors were once more dispatched from the Bridgland head quarters. They were joined by members of the committee in their conclusion that Stratford House would make a perfect new home for the club. A preservation order over the main building was no problem; the club would want to preserve. The east wing, containing the back stairs and the small dining room, could be reorganised for the club's purposes. Birfield wanted £400,000 for Stratford House. The club had most recently been offered only £350,000 for Hanover Square. The ratio was the wrong way round. Bruce and Bridgland divided the task: Bruce would try to reduce the Stratford House price; Bridgland would try to increase the value of Hanover Square. Bridgland reassessed the potential of the old clubhouse site and produced estimates that suggested it could produce sufficient revenue to pay off its own mortgage and that of Stratford House. The operation of rebuilding Hanover Square and buying and refurbishing Stratford House would now cost £1 million,

Sir Arthur Bruce, chairman of the Oriental and saviour of the club 1961-2 .

as opposed to the £800,000 suggested for a move to Chandos House. Bridgland rarely took his eyes from London property price indices. Bruce was having a much more amusing time. He mobilised the human resources of the club; conveniently, one of the members was an old friend of Mr Herbert Hill, chairman of Birfield. The next manoeuvre was easy; lunch at the club. Hill told Bruce that Birfield had recently accepted an offer of £400,000 for Stratford House, that the deal had fallen through, and that Birfield had then refused an offer of £350,000. Some figure in between might be found. Bruce consulted the committee and Bridgland before informing Hill, over lunch, that the club might be able to offer £365,000 subject to approval by an extraordinary general meeting. Hill told him that his directors would accept such an offer and that he looked forward to doing business. Estimates of the costs of Hanover Square's redevelopment and the purchase of Stratford House were now £1,100,000. Hanover Square's value having risen when London County Council agreed to waive its 30 per cent residential requirement in return for full residential use of Stratford House.

Bruce had now to secure short term finance. The club's bank, the Westminster, was not entirely co-operative. One of its joint general managers explained to the dismayed chairman in August, 1960, that the current credit squeeze meant that the bank could not advance, as requested, £1,100,000 over three years but could offer £500,000. The usual sniffy banker's enquiry was made as to long term financial arrangements and repayment of the short term loan. Bruce reminded the bank of previous assurances and their long relationship; the bank wished him luck.

Long term finance, the second leg of the Bridgland plan, was left to the master himself. He played all the aces, having found a tenant for the proposed office block on Hanover Square. In late August, 1960, he telegraphed Bruce, who was on holiday in Sweden, that his old friend the Legal and General Assurance Society was willing to take a long term lease on the new property.

Legal and General would take a head lease with the intention of subletting to subtenants who would have to be found by the club. In September, Legal and General's general manager wrote to Bridgland with detailed plans. The society would pay the equivalent of 14 years of the new block's net income plus £16,000 annual ground rent to the club. Independent assessors reckoned the annual net income of the new building would be £80,000. Consequently, the club would receive a total capital payment of £1,120,000, of which the society would pay £620,000 immediately on the security of Stratford House and the Hanover Square site. Legal and General's main condition was that it make seven per cent annually on its capital outlay.

The bank was much relieved, the committee overjoyed and Sir Ainsley Bridgland typically determined slightly to improve the deal. He was enjoying himself by now and could not resist tinkering to the benefit of the club. The Legal and General would now expect only a 6.5 per cent annual return if the club could find them a single subtenant for the whole block.

Meanwhile, Bruce chaired an extraordinary general meeting which resolved to buy Stratford House; to develop Hanover Square and lease the new premises for no more than 125 years; and to borrow for these purposes up to £1,120,000. Including proxy votes, 844 members voted in favour, five against. The club had a new home; Hanover Square was to be developed; finance was secured in principal: the Bridgland plan was achieved.

ALL BUILDING WORK at Hanover Square and the refurbishment of Stratford House was to be done by Messrs Humphreys Ltd, an established firm of builders chaired by none other than one Sir Aynsley Bridgland. The cost was agreed as the actual expense of the work, estimated by independent auditors, plus a fixed fee of £9,500. Stratford House was actually bought by the Oriental Club on the 2nd of January, 1961. The builders moved in the following day. They had three main tasks. New bedrooms were to be built in the space previously occupied by a great marble ballroom constructed in 1908. A lift was to be installed to give access to them. Finally, the whole building needed redecorating and cleaning.

The total costs of the move to Stratford House, including expenditure in 1962, were:

Freehold	£365,000
Stamp duty and legal fees	£12,108
Architects fees	£11,000
Building contractor	£109,878
Decorating and furnishing	£48,716
Interest on finance (bank)	£37,751
Sundries (engineers etc)	£5,265
	£589,718

Builders were expected to be in for a year and, remarkably, they were on time. The new home of the Oriental Club was opened to its members on new year's day, 1962. Only five had been in the club for its last evening in Hanover Square, a few more came curiously to explore their new habitat on its first day in Stratford House. There were no immediate celebrations or ceremonies, although one of the first parties to be held after the move was in honour of Sir Aynsley Bridgland. Nevertheless, a club in bondage to debt and torpor a few years before had now been led to the promised land.

NUMBER 18, HANOVER Square had been the home of the Oriental Club for 133 years. On the day after members moved to Stratford House the old building was swiftly and mercilessly destroyed. The demolition men were not sentimental.

Construction of the new building was planned to take two years at a cost of £405,000, including Humphrys' fixed fee of £36,000 pounds but excluding architects and engineers. Of course, one more complication threatened the progress of the plan. Part of the plot, the old Conduit Yard, was still occupied by the London Fencing Club which had the lease until 1969. Fortunately the club retained the right to terminate the lease on the 24th of June, 1962, having given 12 months notice. The Oriental offered the swordsmen ample incentive to get out by the end of 1961 but they refused to go. Matters became so unpleasant that Counsel was called in and gave the opinion that the tenants had no right of appeal under the Landlord and Tenant Act and would have to vacate in June with some small compensation from the club.

The London Fencing Club was being bloody-minded for the sake of spite. Reasoning would not work so they were burned out some months before their legally enforced departure. The fire was, of course, entirely accidental and the work of natural justice.

Agreement in principal with Legal and General had been a comparatively simple affair for Bridgland and Bruce, probably involving more lunches. It took 15 months of legal debate for the principles to be reduced to paper; the formal agreement was signed in late March, 1962. Bruce recalled a scintillating read when he composed his memorandum:

It stated, inter alia, that the club would grant to the society a lease of the new property for 120 years; the society would pay to the club a premium of £620,000, and, after the building was let, a ground rent of £16,000 per annum; the society (in order to allow the club to proceed with the letting), would grant back to the club an under-lease for five years at a rent of £43,400 per annum (the equivalent of 7 per cent interest on £620,000); the club would negotiate agreements with one or more tenants on terms to be approved by the society, including rent reviews at not more than 25 year intervals; when the building was fully let, the society would pay to the club such a sum as, together with the initial £620,000, would be equal to [the building's net income minus either an annual allowance of 7 per cent to the society if several tenants were found or 6.5 per cent if the club could find a single tenant to fill the block]; on receipt of the balance of the purchase price, the club would surrender the underlease...

These legal lyrics meant that the club took half the lease price immediately and the other half after the new building was tenanted. If a single tenant could be found then Legal and General would pay slightly more. Lawyers are rarely poets but, to m'learned friends, the agreement was crystalline.

Bruce, still an innocent in the dark ways of property development, was excited by the rent review every 25 years. Could the club raise its income by this method? Bridgland answered him "not without acerbity", explaining that Legal and General might not be so generous if faced with that suggestion, might even pull out all together. The club needed a large capital sum right then, not long term speculation. Any provision for raising rent at the reviews would be "inordinately greedy," said Bridgland. Bruce was suitably contrite.

Once the agreement was signed Legal and General paid the club £620,000 which the club immediately used to pay off its bank loan and overdraft, putting it back in credit after all the expenses of buying and refurbishing Stratford House.

Now, to make the great Bridgland scheme perfect, the club had to find one single tenant to fill the whole of the new Hanover Square office block. This was the only speculative element of the plan: if the club could not find tenants for the new building it would receive a percentage of zero. Bridgland, as always, had the situation in hand.

Back in January, 1961, his acute senses had detected a possible desire by Courtaulds Ltd to move out of their St Martins-le-Grand offices in the City to the West End. That company's subsidiary, British Ceylonese Ltd, already lived at number 22, Hanover Square. Bridgland suggested that number 18 might be available on a 99 year lease at £100,000 per year. Like a hunting tiger stalking its prey, he waited patiently, allowing the idea to ferment for six months. When Bridgland hunted, of course, the kill was inevitable. In August Bruce was again away on holiday - the man was a sybarite - when he received a telegraph from Mr Colclough, the club's solicitor: 'A. B. has hit jackpot with C.,' meaning Aynsley Bridgland had a verbal assent from Courtaulds that it agreed to his terms.

When the building was complete and the tenancy begun, Legal and General would receive its rent of £100,000 per year and pay a capital sum to the club. The rent obtained by Bridgland from Courtaulds, minus Legal and General's 6.5 per cent margin, would deliver to the Oriental Club £1,249,920, of which £620,000 had already been paid. This was a pleasing result for a club which, six years before, had fretted about a £4,700 overdraft.

More complications arose out of Courtaulds' insistence on various architectural features. A director's flat was deemed necessary, along with air-conditioning and double glazing, so the work would now take longer than expected. The true date of completion would be much later than planned. It was made clear that the cost of these alteration, £123,400, would be met by Courtaulds. The rental would run from the original date of completion, as agreed by Courtauld's and the club's architects, so that Courtaulds would pay rent for the six month delay caused by their demands.

In February, 1963, Courtaulds and Legal and General signed an agreement with the Oriental Club, while Courtaulds signed an underlease with Legal and General. Three months remained of the period between the original date of completion and the date required for Courtaulds specifications. For that period Courtaulds paid rent to the club at £100,000 per year; £25,000. After completion, it paid Legal and General which, in turn, on the 15th of May, 1964, paid the club £1,249,400 less the original £620,000 and its legal charges.

Bruce's memorandum analyses the full cost of the Hanover Square development:

Building contractor	£376,188
Stamp duty and legal fees	£28,373
Architects' fees	£22,000
Engineers' fees	£10,000
Estate Agents' fees	£10,000
Sundries	£2,966
Interest (including L&G 'rent')	£106,752
	£556,279
Less rent from Courtaulds	£25,194
	£531,085

Consequently, the total cost to the club of buying Stratford House and building in Hanover Square was £1,114,918. The total receipts from Hanover Square were £1,243,470. The club now enjoyed two freeholds in central London, a beautiful home and a surplus of £128,552.

This surplus was invested to produce, in the mid-60s, an income of around £8,000 per year to add to the ground rent from Hanover Square of £16,000 per year. The capital value of Hanover Square, less the cost of building, turned out to be £912,385, of which £583,833 was spent for Stratford House. The excess £328,552 joined the club's extensive portfolio.

Much more importantly than the dour finance, the move rejuvenated the Oriental Club. Stratford House itself was a much greater attraction than anything in Hanover Square. In 1951 there were 817 members. In 1966 there were 2,376, including 761 associate members.

Luck played a great part in this great escape. The appearence on the market of Stratford House was a blessing; the willingness of Legal and General to buy the lease on such a small margin was a miracle; the intelligence and kindness of Sir Aynsley Bridgland were a proof of human ingenuity and benevolence. He and Bruce were made honorary members and the club made a donation to Bridgland's nominated charity; appropriately for a club to which he had restored all hope, the Samaritans.

The Oriental Club had been saved by the wise advice of two men who knew the value of land: Sir Ainsley Bridgland and the Duke of Wellington. It could now enjoy residence in one of the small palaces of London.

Chapter VII

Stratford House

THE NEW home of the Oriental Club had a beauty far greater than the evolutionary creations of Ben Wyatt or even Decimus Burton in Hanover Square. More than beauty, it had, like many of the beautiful, an interesting past.

Stratford House was 60 years older than the club, built in an age of enlightenment rather than conquest or business, made for decadence rather than function. It was the plaything of an aristocrat, never a very homely home but always the perfect place for a party. The tsar of all the Russias would briefly make his home there. It would be successively a Hapsburg and a Romanov embassy. The ballroom of Stratford House would see some of the first waltzes ever danced in Britain, possibly by the great duke himself, the club's first and only president, a century and a half before the members took it over to ensure that dancing would now be rare. A ghost, that of a suicide lover rejected by her beau, and the mystery of the oxen skulls that decorate the facade and the mantel of the room that served as a bar in the late twentieth century, only add to the intrigue of the building. When the club moved in, Stratford House, for all its youthful beauty, had gained even greater allure for its vast and varied experience.

It was built by a man of great marital shrewdness, possible architectural talent and very little imagination in the naming of buildings. He was, when he purchased the plot, the Honourable Edward Stratford; the property was duly named. Within a few years, and before he was 35 years old, his father had died and he became the second Earl of Aldborough. Still in construction, the property metamorphosed into Aldborough House. Its name would change several times before reverting to the original.

The Stratford family was neither particularly aristocratic nor particularly rich. Heraldic fantasy created the coat of arms that decorates the pediment of Stratford House, arms which the earls claimed to be derived from the sun-burst emblem of Alexander the Great. The first earl was a bog squire in Ireland and member of the Commons for the Wicklow constituency of Baltinglass for over 40 years. He took the barony of Baltinglass in 1763 before, in 1776, when he was over 80 and within months of death, he was promoted to his earldom. The government needed to strengthen its majority in the Lords: Horace Walpole described a "mob of nobility" when, in 17 days, 18 commoners were ennobled, seven barons became viscounts and three of those became earls early the next year. Such wealth as the family had was the result of three generations of men who had assiduously made themselves charming only to the very richest heiresses. Edward Stratford, second Earl of Aldborough, creator of Stratford House, was an eccentric politician, member for Taunton for only a year and, in the Irish Parliament, member for his father's old seat of Baltinglass before he voted that legislature into oblivion with the Act of Union. He was no more nor less romantic than his ancestors, marrying Anne Herbert, grand daughter and grand niece of the eighth and ninth earls of Pembroke, daughter of the Honourable Nicholas Herbert of great Glemham Hall, Suffolk, and an heiress in the fine Stratford tradition.

Aldborough was a visionary and an intellectual. He was the friend of scientists and engineers through his membership of the Royal Society, recipient of a doctorate from Oxford on the day before his own father's funeral, and an enthusiastic builder. Very similar to his house in London was the Aldborough House he built in Dublin, elegant and refined, used in the late twentieth century as a Post Office depository. Equally well made was the model town he created, Stratford-on-Slaney, in the County Wicklow. These achievements and the similarity between them and Stratford House suggest that the earl himself was the main designer, if only in concept, of the London development.

The land had been held by the Corporation of the City of London from the lord of the manor, Gilbert de Sanford, since 1236. It served as a medieval waterworks, collecting from the springs around the old Tyburn River and feeding the pipes that led into the City. Always looking for an excuse to party, the Lord Mayors had held an annual banquet on the site for centuries before Dick Whittington's campanological career decision. "That the feast might be more joyous, And the guests be more contented," the Common Council ordered, on the 18th of September, 1565,

> A good handsome room to be made and built at the conduit heads on this side of Tyburn for the receipt of the Lord Mayor and their Company at the time of the yearly visitation and for the handsome dressing of their meat.

Freehold ownership seems to have passed onto the City from de Sanford's heirs at some point before the Reformation, probably on the suppression of sub-infeudation by the 1290 Statute of *Quia Emptores*. It was certainly owned by the City when Henry VIII acquired it to lease to the Mercers Company in 1514 for six shillings per year. The freehold only returned to the City in 1628 when Charles I gave back

Edward Stratford's town house in the 1780s.

Edward Stratford, second Earl of Aldborough, builder of Stratford Place.

the land as part payment of a debt. The value was reckoned to be 36 years rent at £8 per year; 150 years before Stratford House was built its site was worth only £288.

By the early eighteenth century the feast had moved to more convenient premises and the Banqueting House was derelict. In 1736, three years before the construction of the Lord Mayor's modern Mansion House, the old ruins were sold off for timber, realising £18. The site was let as pasture to Henry Warrington for £14 per year; he sublet to George Shakespeare. His gentle kine chewed the cud, much in the way of later inhabitants, for 35 years.

Then, on Wednesday, the 5th of June, 1771, the Common Council of the City of London was propositioned:

> The Humble Petition of the Honble. Edward Stratford
> of Dean Street, Soho, sheweth
>
> That your Petitioner is informed that the City are possessed of a piece of ground on the north side of Oxford Road commonly called or known by the name of Lord Mayor's Banqueting House Ground, part of the City Mead Estate now occupied by Mr George Shakespeare for a term Which is near expiring and your Petitioner conceives will admit of great improvement by erecting new buildings thereon.
>
> That your Petitioner apprehends if the said piece of land was properly laid out and good Buildings erected upon it, it would not only be a great advantage to the City, but an Ornament to the rest of the City Mead Estate and as your Petitioner is desirous of embarking on the said undertaking and will give the full value of the premes,
>
> YOUR PETITIONER THEREFORE HUMBLY PRAYS:
>
> this Honourable Court will be pleased to grant him
> a Building Renewable Lease thereof on such terms
> and conditions as shall be thought fit.
>
> And your Petitioner will ever pray,
> etc.
>
> *EDWARD STRATFORD.*

The terms and conditions that were eventually thought fit were negotiated with a Corporation subcommittee chaired by George Dance, architect of the lost Newgate Gaol and tutor of the great John Soane. It was agreed that Stratford would pay the City an annual rent of £160, renewable every 14 years on payment of a fine of five years' ground rent.

The appropriate aristocrat now possessed the perfect plot. He almost certainly knew what he wanted; not only did he have a designer's imagination but also an engineer's practicality. An almost contemporary observer of his work on Aldborough House in Dublin commented that it was built, "on a very fanciful plan, agreeable to his Lordship's own views." Moreover, his wife was from a family of keen architectural connoisseurs. Yet they were still amateurs while Stratford House and the original scheme for all of Stratford Place were certainly the work of a professional.

His identity is mysterious. The drawings attached to the lease are unsigned and the originals lost. Style and period suggest that the Adam brothers might have been involved. That happy speculation is unlikely to be true because Stratford House does not quite display their economy of space, because the brothers' own archives make no mention of it and because, in a country full of eighteenth century mansions, a couple of Ionic capitols do not automatically earn their authorship.

A more likely candidate is Richard Edwin, the young pupil of Matthew Brettingham, the most fashionable architect of the day. While still a student, his detail drawing of Inigo Jones's Water Gate at York Place won him the Royal Society of Arts Premium in the Polite Arts; clearly a latter-day good mannerist. He competed for the commission for a new Royal Exchange in Dublin and submitted drawings to the Society of Artists of Great Britain of a 'Design for a Temple.' Edwin had strong Stratford connections. He represented Stratford at least twice at the Corporation sub-committee that considered the humble petition. One of the drawings he offered to the Royal Academy was 'A Longitudinal Elevation of the West Side of Stratford Place, Oxford Street'. Finally, when Stratford Place was complete he moved into number five, on the east side.

The evidence is circumstantial; probably not enough to convict beyond reasonable doubt but persuasive on the balance of probabilities. If Richard Edwin was the architect of Stratford Place then the loss was only greater when he died in 1778, only 32 years old.

The subcommittee was very happy with the plans, who ever was their author. Stratford Place, they said, would be

...equal to, if not exceed, the most magnificent structures of Europe.

St Sofia and Chartres could clearly never compete with Stratford Place. The subcommittee members were more prosaic later in their opinions. Quoting the sum suggested by Stratford, they said that the appearance of the buildings were not all that important

...providing the sum of £40,000 was laid out in erecting good, substantial dwelling places.

The work proved to be magnificent, good and substantial. During their site inspection of 1774 members of the subcommittee complained that the plans had clearly changed. They were satisfied when Stratford carefully explained how the emendations were vastly superior to the first drafts.

In his enthusiasm, Stratford managed to annex a little more *lebensraum* than was strictly his to build upon. The first such invasion of another's property was quickly resolved; Mr Gee, the invaded landlord, conveniently died in 1772 and, like an Anatolian king to Rome, he left the ground in question to Stratford. The second encroachment was down the west side of the place where parts of Stratford's building verged across the line onto the land of Thomas Hope. Settlement was achieved only after 60 years: Thomas Smith, in his *The Parish of St Mary-le-Bone* (1833), explained that Stratford,

...who in his anxiety to render Stratford Place the most magnificent pile of buildings of that period, made a still further encroachment on this estate by erecting the buildings on the west side of Stratford Place, over the brook which formed the boundary line between the two estates, but for which compensation has recently been made.

No doubt other such problems accumulated. Whatever the wealth of the countess, the development of Stratford Place was no small financial outlay. Stratford's bankers, Messrs Mayne & Company, wrote to him on the 4th of December, 1776, suggesting a "present scarcity of cash" and requesting him to put his account in order, a request that required £3,192, 12s, 11d. Five years later he transferred the lease of Stratford House itself, now called Aldborough like himself, into the name of his wife who had, obligingly, already lent him £10,000.

Nevertheless, the development continued. Some of the residents of Stratford Place paid for the work on their houses themselves. They included a member of Parliament, Sir George Yonge, and the Earl Poulett. The noble tenant later moved to Hanover Square where his countess frequently complained of her garden being ruined by the soot from the Oriental Club's kitchens. Stratford was still in financial trouble. In May, 1775, he had to raise £2,000 by transferring title to six houses in the Place to a certain Mrs Ann Wood.

Edward Stratford, Earl of Aldborough did manage to realise his dream of living in the beautiful Stratford, then Aldborough House he had created in London. He and his generous wife divided their time between there and their estates in Ireland until 1785. Then the Countess Aldborough died unexpectedly. The earl decided to move to the house he had envisioned as a dower, number 12, next door, rather than continue alone in his palace.

The great house now started its long career for rent.

THE ULTIMATE landlord remained the Corporation of the City of London but the real squire of Stratford Place, the holder of the renewable lease, was still Edward Stratford, Earl of Aldborough. The great house was first tenanted by an undistinguished lawyer who had sufficient place at court to become the Earl Talbot in 1786. He was the Lord Steward of England, a minor patron of the arts, famously generous host and dead, at 43, in 1793. His wife kept the house until 1797 when she moved to an increasingly glamorous address in Hanover Square.

Meanwhile, the widowered Earl of Aldborough next door had remembered the sources of the Stratford fortune and, like some figment of the imagination of Jane Austen, he went to Bath. There he found another heiress, Miss Elizabeth Henniker, with £50,000. They were married within a year of the death of the first countess, enjoyed a short grand tour and returned to London to play at court, becoming great friends of the future Prince Regent and Mrs Fitzherbert. That morganatic wife would find her nemesis in Stratford House several years later. Now, on the departure of Lady Talbot, the house was let for the year 1797 to 1798 to a diplomat and prominent member of the Carlton House set, Robert Adair.

He was followed by the Earl of Jersey. An earl's coronet seemed to send men scurrying to Stratford Place in the early years. This belted nobleman's consort was a woman of sufficient beauty and bad taste to replace Mrs Fitzherbert in the affections of the Prince of Wales. Prinny was a frequent visitor, Stratford House the scene of much rotund royal copulation and all the more convenient because the princely

Priapus could call on his friend Richard Cosway at number 19, Stratford Place, a famous miniaturist, fop and libertine.

The second Earl of Aldborough died on the 2nd of January, 1801, leaving no children. His brother inherited, as did another before the line died out on the death of the seventh earl in 1875. Stratford House did not go to the earls. Aldborough's older sister had married Lord Powerscourt (Restoration comedy could not invent these names) to produce twin sons, one of whom, Lieutenant-Colonel John Wingfield-Stratford, now inherited the renewable lease. Aldborough's second wife quickly married a barrister, dangerous but rarely fatal husbands, before herself dying within a year. The dower-house, number 12, was retained by her widower.

When, in 1805, the Earl of Jersey died, his widow chose to sell the remainder of their lease to his cousin the Duke of St Albans. He was another court functionary with a Savoyard title; Hereditary Grand Falconer of England. Appropriately feather brained, the Duke was useful to the Foreign Office during the great conferences after the battles of Leipzig and Waterloo. A Hungarian grandee, Prince Paul Esterhazy, needed to find lodgings for two visiting Austrian archdukes, John and Louis. Stratford House, now, inevitably, St Albans House, was the perfect billet and the duke was agreeable. Napoleon's 100 days in 1815 delayed the visit long enough to prevent the duke from ever meeting his guests. He died on the 15 of August, 1815, the day before Esterhazy was appointed ambassador to the Court of St James.

The archdukes arrived in mid-October, made their courtly calls to various palaces and found themselves whisked off on a tour of early industrial Britain. They grew used to the speeches of aldermen while Esterhazy enjoyed, uninterrupted, the delights of Stratford House. When the two Hapsburgs returned to Vienna, Esterhazy stayed on in the house while his new embassy was being fitted out at Chandos House, a potential home of the Oriental Club 145 years later. The prince assiduously followed Metternich's instructions to flatter the Prince Regent who returned to Stratford House for innumerable balls and dinners and, doubtless, the occasional assignation.

St. Albans had entertained royalty in the house some time before. When Tsar Alexander visited London in 1814 he was accompanied by a vast retinue including one lowly attachè, Leopold of Saxe-Coburg. Only slightly royal and very junior, he stayed in an apartment above Mr Hole's grocery store for three guineas without candles. Much later, when he was a little more important, he recalled the story in a letter to his niece, Queen Victoria, referring to himself in the third person:

I forgot to mention a subject which has been since told as a proof of the great poverty of Prince Leopold when he was in England in 1814. He came with the Emperor Alexander, and as long as the Emperor remained himself in England, the lodgings of the persons who had come with him were paid by him. The Russian Ambassador, Count Lieven, had the charge of locating the suite, and as they lived in Harley Street they lodged the people near it, and had taken a rather indifferent lodging for Prince Leopold in High Street, Marylebone. The Prince had nothing to do with the choice of that lodging, and as soon as the Emperor had left, he lodged himself in Stratford Place, in a House where General Count Beroldingen, the Wurtenberg Minister, lodged, and where he remained till he left England.

Beroldingen had in fact taken rooms for the summer in Stratford House. Leopold returned there three years later, just before the archdukes departed. He had come to London at the invitation of the Regent, who wanted him to marry his daughter Charlotte. It was an important mission: the girl was heir to the throne. Nobody bothered to find appropriate accommodation for the man expected to perpetuate the dynasty, so Count Munster, the Hanovarian minister, found him a single room in Bond Street. No breakfast was served and the Prince was forced to beg for his eggs and bacon from the archdukes at Stratford House.

The usual politics and bitchiness of Regency life abounded. Perhaps the archdukes were not fascinating but one guest at least underestimated Esterhazy, one of the creators of the five power system that allowed Russia, Austria-Hungary, Prussia-Germany, France and Britain to maintain peace for 99 years. Lady Harriet Granville wrote to her sister Lady Morpeth early in 1816:

> We dined there [Stratford House] on Sunday. It was a dinner quite unrivalled in the records of dullness. The archdukes scarcely utter, though the eldest looks intelligent, but the youngest is without vivacity, and it is said they are as bored as they look... Esterhazy crowned this flow of soul. He is silly and tiresome to the supremest degree.

Lady Harriet really did not approve of the Magyar prince:

> He is clever but he is childish, and I do not like little boys of 34.

She offered only a "hostile and perfidious politeness" to his "small, round, black" wife. When they left Stratford House in March, 1817, their replacements were much more acceptable to society matrons. The new chatelaine was the woman who had treated poor Prince Leopold so shabbily on his first visit, Princess Lieven, wife of the Russian ambassador. Lady Harriet shared her approval with Lady Morpeth:

> Madame Lieven, whom you enquired about, is become famous for civility and empressements to everyone.

Lieven and Esterhazy were the two most important members of the diplomatic corps: the Turks were largely irrelevant to the post-Napoleonic settlement; the Germans were still represented by fractured principalities; the French were in no position to ask for anything and nobody cared what the embryonic, upstart Americans thought. It is likely that much of the work that defined nineteenth century Europe was done in Stratford House.

Its Russian mistress had an immediate problem. While she and her husband stayed at the Harley Street residence the princess had to find a house suitable for Grand Duke Nicholas, brother of Tsar Alexander I. No Marylebone hovel would do for this heroic warrior and heir to his childless brother's crown. Within weeks of the Hapsburg departure the Romanovs were comfortably settled in Stratford House. The grand duke was not a charming man; he had a "mania for uniforms" according to Princess Lieven. Less charming even than that, was the possibility that he had conspired with his brother to murder their father, the 'mad Tsar' Paul I.

Stratford Place as originally designed.

Elevations of the front and sides of the Place never came off the drawing board.

Nicholas himself came to the throne in 1825 under strange circumstances. Alexander died mysteriously in Siberia. Rumours persisted that he was still alive, having retired to the tundra as a hermit known as Feodor Kusmitch, who lived until 1864. To prove the legitimacy of his reign, Nicholas had his brother's coffin opened. It was empty.

He went on to become a fierce, reactionary ruler dedicated to 'Autocracy, Orthodoxy and Nationalism'. During his time at Stratford House, however, he put it to the purpose for which it was designed and threw parties. The great dandy Thomas Raikes recalled the dancing in his *A Visit to St Petersburg, 1824-30,* which he probably heard from his home at number 5, Stratford Place:

> You may remember the present Emperor Nicholas fourteen years ago in London, when he lived in the large house at the end of Stratford Place... He was then one of the Grand Dukes of Russia, travelling for his amusement; a fine looking youth, making a conspicuous figure in the waltz, and whirling our English beauties round the circle to a quicker movement than they had previously learned to practice.

Nicholas went on travelling for his amusement in the early summer of 1818, but he was succeeded at Stratford House by his younger brothers the Grand Dukes John and Michael. By the end of the year Princess Lieven had set them on their way to further tours of foundries and town halls. Stratford House had one more dynast to entertain. Yet another archduke, Archduke Maximillian of Austria, now took up residence at the suggestion of the Esterhazys. He stayed until late 1819 when he left to endure the usual municipal fate of foreign aristocrats in Regency England.

Now, for the first time, Stratford House would be a family home.

ENGLISH LAND law was completely reformed in 1925 to make it merely opaque. Before that it was incomprehensible. When Archduke Maximillian moved out in 1819, the freehold of Stratford House was owned by the Lord Mayor and Corporation of the City of London. The long renewable lease was held by the heavily hyphenated Lieutenant-Colonel Wingfield-Stratford, who had inherited it from his uncle, the second Earl of Aldborough. Wingfield-Stratford's lease was sub-let to the Earl of Jersey, whose widowed countess had resub-let to the Duke of St Albans, whose heirs had, in turn, resub-let to the various embassies and the wilting flower of European nobility. Nothing could be simpler; the legal situation was transparent *con aqua et terra,* as they say in Chancery.

Now, in 1819, the lease held by the Jerseys came to an end and possession of Stratford House reverted to Colonel Wingfield-Stratford. He had already purchased number 12, the dower house, from the barrister who had married Aldborough's second wife and widow and inherited on her death. The Wingfield-Stratfords moved into the big house, releasing the great state rooms as playgrounds for their brood; young John, Frances and Isabel. They had vast territories to explore. The Oriental Club's bar was the dining room, square as it was in the late twentieth century but with a wide alcove that stretched its walls back to the library, which has always served a bookish purpose. The cube to the west of the library was a morning room and the club's billiard room provided a spare parlour. The grandest rooms were above. The club's main drawing room was the location of diplomatic balls, scene of a future tsar's rapid waltzing. The barrel roofed chamber above the front door was the main drawing room. If Edwin was the architect, he prized form over function: the great public rooms designed to be used in the evening take all the southern sunlight while the private rooms, used in the day face the gloomy north. The club's smoking room, always in two sections, were the main bedrooms. Apart from further bedrooms and nurseries aloft, that was the extent of Stratford House. The club's modern dining room and the rooms above it occupy space then used as stables. Overwhelmingly undomestic, Stratford House was made for splendour not for comfort.

Tragedy struck the Wingfield-Stratfords in 1829. They left the house when the colonel's wife died appallingly young. The family stayed in Stratford Place, first at number nine, then in the old dower house at number 12.

Their successor in the big house was an old-fashioned Tory politician from Yorkshire, Sir John Beckett. Strangely, he had two connections with the Oriental Club without ever being a member. Firstly, his brother-in-law was the great Lord William Bentinck, one of the clan that remade India and one of Malcolm's gathering that founded the club. Secondly, he was a political ally of the Duke of Wellington, serving with him in the cabinets between 1823 and 1830. The Duke, an Irishman of the Protestant Ascendancy, could not tolerate Beckett's views on Catholic emancipation in the early thirties, but before then he was a frequent visitor to Stratford House. The building that would house the Oriental Club had often entertained its first and only president.

Beckett died in 1847. His wife ended her days there in 1871. During her old age she was blind and agoraphobic. She wandered around the darkened house only ever leaving to walk through the garden by the guidance of a handrail, enjoying the perfume of her roses.

Anne Beckett bequeathed Stratford House to her nephew, George Bentinck MP, a member of the Oriental, related to the great Indian governors, and utterly confused as to what to do with an urban mansion. The Beckett's lease from the Wingfield-Stratfords still had many years to run and Bentinck was in no need of shelter. His problem was solved when his brother-in-law, John Leslie of the County Monaghan, offered to buy the remainder of the lease. Records of the price are elusive but Forrest, whose research is deep, reports a tradition of a sum 'under nine thousand pounds'.

Again, a family lived in Stratford House, and a grand one. Leslie's money was safe in vast estates in Ireland. He had a grand house within his demesne at Castle Leslie in Glasough and, until his move to Stratford House, a famous salon down the road in Berkeley Square. Land owning Anglo-Irishmen did not actually need a job. Leslie occupied himself by ensuring that his tenants made him £20,000 per year without any of the usual Irish hardship. He was a benevolent absentee and his estates were famous for humanity towards his dependants.

His London home, so long the dark haunt of a sightless widow, now became a glittering centre of the capital's social whirl, embellished by his children; Mary, Constance, Dosia, Olive and poor out-numbered Jack, whose marriage made him an uncle of Winston Churchill. Family unity was so tight that Stratford House was the place of one of the boy Churchill's happiest moments; meeting a particular hero, the writer Sir Henry Ryder Haggard.

The beautiful people came to Stratford House; all the leaders of the arts, literature, music, the peerage and consistently Tory politics were entertained. Benjamin Disraeli, who had given Leslie a baronetcy, climbed to the top of the staircase, looked around, turned to Lady Constance Leslie and gasped "Vistas!" He exaggerated, as he often did, but he proved that the family was worth flattering. A scion, the writer Sir Shane Leslie, reminisced in 1900 of decades long past:

> Called on Mrs Leslie in her glorious old house in Stratford Place, which is beautiful because all the colour is subdued, no new gilding or smartness. She herself sat in the window embroidering, with the bright sunlight just glinting on her rippled hair and sweet face, at once a picture and a poem.

The whole house stank. Sir Shane also wrote of a permanent and disgusting smell. Irish footmen, used to the cold, wet air of Monaghan, were imported for the summer social season. They quickly fell ill and several died. The Leslie's, who must have had no olfactory senses, were sufficiently curious to investigate the plumbing. Stratford House did not relegate its raw sewage to the drains of London, it was discovered, but to one enormous, saturated pit under the main staircase. Richard Edwin, chief suspect for the architecture, was not as good at hygiene as he was at aesthetics. The Leslies were made of sterner stuff than their footmen; they resolutely ignored the odour of ordure, and expected any visiting prime ministers to do the same. Of course, unlike the footmen, they did not have to live in the basement.

The land law complications over Stratford House were simplified in 1883. Colonel Wingfield-Stratford's heir died in 1881. His son, another Edward, was the sort of man who would have been welcome at any gathering of the Oriental Club until he asked for credit. His gambling was vigorous and unlucky. In two years he lost his family's estates in Ireland and Kent and found it necessary to sell his renewable lease on Stratford House. The Leslies obliged. The Corporation of the City of London still had the freehold of the ground, a small ground-rent was still payable, but now the possessors and residents of Stratford House were once again tenants-in-chief. The house's connection with the Stratford family had ended.

The Leslies grew old in Stratford House. They saw all their children make illustrious marriages and devoted their home to public celebration and domestic affection. Eventually, in 1894, they moved on to a smaller house in Manchester Square. Sir John lived until 1916 so that his grandson Seymour Leslie could accurately write that "he who had talked to Walter Scott on a mail coach lived to see and hear the first air raids." They gave Stratford House to their son-in-law, a banker and member of Parliament, Walter Murray Guthrie, chairman of Chalmers, Guthrie & Company. In the late twentieth century one of his descendants held Wellington's old job; Field Marshal Sir Charles Guthrie was chief of the general staff in the 1990s. Walter Guthrie tried to pay the Leslies £16,000 but they never presented the cheque.

The new regime was as glamorous as the old; the Stratford House party continued. Meanwhile, Guthrie made some important changes to the fabric of the house. With understandable dispatch, the pit beneath the stairs was replaced by London's magnificent sewage system. More obviously, to the eye at least, the wings that project east from the Oriental's bar and west from the Oriental's cloakroom had only ever been single story, elegant colonnades used for stabling or servant accommodation. He put another floor above them to provide a few gracious bedrooms. The wings, connecting the house to the sides of Stratford Place, were still two stories lower than the centre of the building, but the alteration provided necessary extra space.

Old houses deserve neither status nor respect unless they are adequately equipped with either buried treasure or a ghost. Fortunately, Guthrie managed to supply Stratford House with a regulation phantom. He had many lovers and, inevitably, broke

Lord Derby's 1908 ballroom, later converted to bedrooms.

Lord and Lady Colebrooke kept a cluttered drawing room from 1902 to 1908.

a few hearts. One girl took it all far too seriously and attempted suicide. She failed. Guthrie outlived her, however, so that he woke one night in Stratford House to see her shade, the noose incompetently knotted about her neck, weeping beside his bed. She has reappeared many times in the upper floors, an unhappy spectre for a house so used to joviality. The victim of love, she has, no doubt, appreciated the companionship of the Oriental Club; a few members, no doubt, have welcomed a lonely succuba.

During the Guthries' time at Stratford Place the kitchens were blessed by the cuisine of Rosa Lewis, the most famous chef of the time. She went on to cook at Whites, a position to which she was helped by her old employer who wrote to her that:

> I shall do all in my power to make it a success. I am sure that your own personality will do that without any outside help.

It was quite a personality; sufficient to make her a mistress of the Prince of Wales, a necessary liaison for all ladies of fashion, and to get her fired from Whites for calling a committee member a "a damned old woodcock in tights," an eccentric garment for a gentleman in the 1890s. Two years later she bought the Cavendish Hotel and gave it a reputation for the best cuisine in the land.

Sated by her food and exhausted by the social life, Guthrie gave up Stratford House in 1902. The new owner of the City's long, cheap renewable lease was the son, grandson and great grandson of Indian administrators and Oriental Club members. His grand-father was a committee member in 1825 as well as a judge of the Court of Appeal in Calcutta and a pioneer in the study of Sanskrit. Lord Edward Colebrooke, who now moved in, was another court functionary. His wife was a god-daughter of the Princess of Wales and he took his barony and the office of a lord-in-waiting from this proximity to the throne. His new home once more sheltered the grandest social occasions in London.

The house benefited from three minor alterations by Colebrooke. First, a lift was installed for those who found the grand staircase intimidating. Second, the library was completely redesigned. The only perfect double cube room in London was given a very good imitation of the Adam style to confuse even more those seeking the identity of the house's architect. The exquisite mahogany and ormolu demonstrate the wealth and artistry available to Colebrooke. Third, the garden, neglected by the Guthries, was again filled with roses.

Forrest had first-hand evidence of Stratford House at the time:

> ...in December 1967 I had the pleasure of walking round Stratford House with Lord Colebrooke's daughter, the Honourable Lady Packe, who spent several years of her girlhood there. She told me that, like so many of the children of grand houses in those days, her life was lived almost entirely apart from the grown-ups; there were only occasional descents from the schoolroom to the drawing room, the library or her mother's first floor bedroom.

When the Colebrookes moved away in 1908 Stratford House exercised its old magnetism and attracted yet another earl.

THE NOBLE moth that next touched the Stratford flame was the seventeenth Earl of Derby, a distinguished politician, patrician magnate, and great land owner who served in the coalition cabinets of the man who most damaged the plutocracy of the aristocracy, David Lloyd George. In politics, Derby had the luxury of independent wealth; he seemed unambitious because he had nothing much to gain and little desire to pander to any caucus that might have supported him. It was almost a pleasing hobby in which, quite understandably, he saw no reason to take instruction.

He had perfectly adequate premises on St James's Square but he was there hemmed in, as so many have been, by an inconsiderate Bishop of London. Stratford Place had building space, and Derby wanted extensions.

He was accustomed to spacious living and determined to make Disraeli's 'vistas' reality. Stratford House, now, of course, Derby House, seemed cramped; the earl famously wondered:

How ever a big family got into this house I do not know.

Rebuilding became necessary and possible for two reasons. The house would be required for political hospitality. Consequently several rooms and access to them were needed so that the occupants of one might not know of the presence of the occupants of the other. More space yet was allowed by the introduction of the infernal combustion engine and the obsolescence of stables.

The old stables to the east were replaced by a state dining room on the ground floor, later the club's dining room, and a great ballroom on the first floor, which would be destroyed half a century later. The symmetry of the Stratford Place facade was maintained by the building of further floors on the wings of the house to make a uniform roof level and provide extra bedrooms and more comfortable accommodation for the staff. From the front, the modern Oriental Club is as Derby left it, and behind, the club's small dining room and the whole construction to the east of the courtyard were the work of the Earl. Further construction within the original building allowed various furniture and fittings to be moved from the St James's Square house, including the fireplaces from an older Derby House, in Grosvenor Square, designed by Robert Adam in 1774.

Only one of Derby's alterations may be regretted. The original staircase, no longer over its midden, had consisted of a central flight to a landing half way to the first floor and two flights up from the landing set against the north and south walls of the lobby. Above, a gallery from the upper floors lined the tall walls beneath the great, domed skylight. This escalation was, like most of Stratford House, designed for partying; it was perfect for the dramatic, sweeping entrance.

Derby destroyed symmetry. One flight against the south wall now climbed to the landing and a single second flight against the north wall. The gallery, always an interesting perch for discreet observers, was lost to high mirrored windows of the French style, perfect for capturing the light that poured in from above. These are the constructions that would survive to elevate and illuminate members of the Oriental Club.

The first architects commissioned for the work were old friends of the Oriental. The firm of MacVicar Anderson had been one of those asked to make plans for the usual, heavy alterations to Hanover Square during the 1880s; plans which, as usual, proved financially impossible. Derby did not approve of their Stratford House drawings and called in Romaine-Walker and Besant, a very fashionable firm, which provided the final scheme. The substitute's work, the surviving facade, was much more sympathetic to the original vision of Stratford and Edwin than MacVicar Anderson's alternative which would have made Stratford House look like a building society.

It was to provide shelter on two of the most momentous occasions of London life in 1911 and 1916. New kings are excuses for celebration. Even if George V was not blessed with social aplomb, his succession must be duly recognised. In 1911 Stratford House saw its greatest party since the days of Grand Duke Nicholas. On the 27th of June Lady Derby entertained eight imperial highnesses, 32 royal highnesses and only one commoner. That unfortunate lowborn was Mr Whitelaw Reid, descendent of treacherous revolutionaries and American ambassador to the Court of St James. Only nine countries sent full ambassadors to London then, six were at the party; Turkey, Italy and Germany sent their apologies.

Five years later, on the 5th of December, 1916, a more sombre group gathered for breakfast in the new small dining room. Joining their host, Winston Churchill, David Lloyd George, Andrew Bonar Law and Edward Carson munched their marmalade and discussed the downfall of the prime minister. Later that day Derby and Lloyd George resigned from the cabinet to form the unofficial opposition that forced Asquith's resignation.

Derby still continued to work as an active politician, fully enjoying the fruits of his alliance with the Welsh wizard. The centre of his activity in Stratford House was the old dining room, freed by his extensions to become his study. Keen to keep in touch in an age of several daily postal deliveries, he would sit at the front window, waiting for his correspondence to be passed straight through to him by the postman with a friendly word or, for the unpunctual, a terrible wrath. His wealth, mostly in industry and land in Lancashire became his main preoccupation as the twenties rolled on so that by 1930 he hardly used the London house. Asked why he bothered to keep it at all he answered:

> Well, Lady Derby must have somewhere to change when she comes up from Coworth to go to the play.

The countess's love of theatre was sufficient to maintain Derby's interest in the ownership of Stratford House. When he had moved in, in 1908, he had bought the ground's long renewable lease, becoming the tenant-in-chief of the City of London. In 1930 he started negotiations with the City Lands Committee of the Corporation. After much work, terms were agreed: 75 years purchase at £8 on the house, £2 on the old stables and coach houses, and £5 for the pavement in front on Stratford Place. Fifteen pounds multiplied by 75 allowed Derby to buy Stratford House outright for £1,125. The offer was accepted by the Common Council on the 17th of March, 1932. The Lord Mayor and Corporation of the City of London had owned the site for 696 years. Now its inhabitants, possessors and full owners were united in the Earl of Derby so that Stratford House could be fully and freely disposed of.

DURING THE Second World War Derby finally decided that he had no further need of Stratford House. The great building's existence as a private home was ended. Derby's great art collection was shipped to safety from the bombs to Druce's

Guthrie raised the wings of Stratford House by one floor in the 1890s.

Depository on Baker Street where it was promptly destroyed by a particularly philistine German bombardier. Stratford House, unscathed, lay empty.

A 'for sale' sign was hoisted, but few people would buy property in London while the bombs still fell. Derby's old friend, Sir Alec Martin, provided a perfect way to fill the wasted space.

The Luftwaffe's art appreciation training was severely tested during the Second World War. Christies was bombed to rubble during April, 1941. Martin was managing director of the auction house as well as artistic advisor to Derby. He now had an auction of stamps for the Red Cross to conduct and nowhere to conduct it. Derby was keen to help, telegraphing his response to Martin's request to use Stratford House:

> Certainly, and if any use afterwards to Christies, go there.

It was much use afterwards. Christies were given the use of Stratford House rent-free for the duration of the war and six months of peace; fine treasures were knocked down in the great ballroom. The finest, perhaps, was *The Young Waltonians,* a Constable sold to Mr Walter Hutchinson for £41,000.

Martin would have liked to lease and make Stratford House the home of Christies but Derby was determined to sell. When a faceless financial consortium bought the house he almost managed to take a lease from the new owners but, in 1946, they very quickly sold on the freehold. Stratford House had clearly affected the new buyer when he had visited its auction rooms; he was Martin's old client, Walter Hutchinson. Christies stayed on until Lord Spencer offered his house in St James's, and then moved back to their rebuilt premises in 1953.

Like Christies, Hutchinson's publishing group had been bombed out, its building in Paternoster Row destroyed in the great raids of December, 1941. The big house at the end of Stratford Place was a testimony to the egotism of two centuries of London landowners: it now became Hutchinson House. As well as providing office space, it became the venue of one of Hutchinson's more eccentric projects. He was a great sportsman, a lover of gun and rod, and thought himself a great connoisseur of art. The two enthusiasms were combined in the National Gallery of British Sports and Pastimes, the collection of which now shared Stratford House with Hutchinson's publishing staff.

A curator was hired to choose the best from Hutchinson's collection of 3,000 works. Mr John Wheatley ARA, formerly of Sheffield Art Gallery, selected 560 of the best and revealed them to the public in February, 1949. The walls were festooned with racing, hunting, fishing, shooting and a vast amount of slaughtered fauna. *The Young Waltonians* just about qualified as a depiction of sports or pastimes because it includes some children fishing; in the gallery it was catalogued, very appropriately for its new home, as *Stratford Mill by the Stour,* and hung in the place of honour, roped off at the end of the ballroom.

Hutchinson died in 1950, leaving the gallery without a patron or a chance of survival. It did not quite last two years. It did not have the sufficient public interest or artistic quality to continue without the potent caprice of its idiosyncratic founder. On the 1st of June, 1951, Country Life explained its failure: it was:

> ...too ambitious and on insufficiently selective lines.

The Stubbs's and the Morlands and, of course, the Constable were sold off but Hutchinson's companies remained for another four years. The occasional wedding or other celebration was held in the main rooms, the house's original purpose of partying was never forgotten, but it was declining into an office block with a classical facade.

In 1955 Birfield Ltd bought Stratford House. It was the nadir of the great mansion's life. Forrest, who remembered Hutchinson's gallery but never saw the Birfield corporate vandalism, felt the insult to the building:

> Aesthetically, too, is there anything more wretched than an eighteenth century drawing room with a row of green filing cabinets jostling the Adam chimney piece and strip lights hanging from the stuccoed ceiling? Better concrete, steel, and fitness of purpose!

Any Adam chimney pieces were Derby contributions but the stuccoed ceilings had looked down on men who knew how to appreciate Stratford House. The Dukes, Arch Dukes, Grand Dukes, the Tsar, the ambassadors, the princes and princesses, the Regent and his lovers, and all the endless earls, including the second Earl of Aldborough, would have found the utilitarian, tedious offices confusing and despicable. Their old home, a place of hospitality and careless celebration, had been turned into a machine of humanity.

The Oriental Club and Stratford House saved each others' souls.

Chapter VIII

Renaissance

FOR THE first time in its life, the Oriental Club now had a healthy membership, in numbers as well as life-expectancy, and sound finances. The freehold and fixed income from Hanover Square combined with a safe share portfolio to provide rare security. Stratford House attracted vigorous new members, happy to visit the club often and spend gratifying amounts of treasure in the precincts of its splendid new palace. A sick old elephant had polished her tusks and raised her trunk in triumphant salute.

Members were quick to exploit their new home. Strip lighting and filing cabinets were soon removed to leave Stratford House much as Lord Derby had left it. One new structural alteration was required to change his mansion into a comfortable and practical clubhouse. A large part of the club's income and a fundamental benefit to its members came from accommodation. The great marbled ballroom of 1908, in which the Countess of Derby had danced to celebrate the accession of George V and Christies had knocked down treasure, would now ravel up the sleeve of care. Of the money spent on refurbishing Stratford House, most converted that high-pillared chamber into two floors of bedrooms. A lift door was installed by the dining room to carry luggage and heavy members to their beds. Derby's grand ceiling was not destroyed. In the late 1990s it could still be seen in the roof spaces.

Further bedrooms were installed in the attics and lofts behind Stratford's great facade so that, for the same price, members might find themselves in a comparatively grand apartment once occupied by a member of Derby's family or a comfortable box once occupied by several of his large staff.

Sir Arthur Bruce's memorandum on the great move thanks his vice-chairman, the Earl of Inchcape, for all his service and ingenuity but especially for...

arranging with Mssrs Leggatt Brothers for the cutting, cleaning, reframing and hanging of the pictures - a difficult operation which was achieved with very felicitous results.

Difficult and heart-breaking, with very obscene results. The paintings were cut severely from the full works that decorated the high and wide acres of wall space in Hanover Square to the busts that hang in Stratford House. Before the brutal bayonets of Mssrs Leggatt Brothers cut the canvass these were magnificent works, if not always for their artistic value then for their historical detail and the deserved compliment paid to their subjects by their grandeur. Malcolm and King stood respectively in the full scapes of a Persian desert or a heaving quarter-deck. Tippu Sultan looked down on members from the heights of his Seringapatam citadel, Cornwallis surrounded by the guns destroyed by the forces of a treacherous Virginian colonel, Clive beside his colours from Plassey and Hastings behind a desk covered in the papers of his cleansing regime. Inchcape sliced away pyramids and palaces, pikestaffs and palanquins. The art was of different proportions to the new clubhouse so, of course, the art must be mutilated. If Inchcape did not respect painting he might have sold the collection to those who did, with the space and the eye to appreciate the works, and used the money to buy portraits of the same subjects, images with the same themes appropriate to the club and proportionate to its new home.

Nevertheless, the club in Stratford House was left its *lares et penates,* its household gods, quadriplegics in gold and scarlet, still tolerant in their protective and benign gaze. A short journey across London had cost the pathfinders of the British in the Orient their limbs and their perspective, and a few of their decorations, but they remained forgiving, familiar companions to their successors. The club commissioned a portrait of the Earl of Inchcape in November, 1982.

By the mid-1950s fewer members were really direct successors of the oily characters on the walls. Since the last Alfred Club member had died the membership had slightly moved back to its old eastern bias. Occidentals were always welcome, as Sir Alfred Pickford pointed out in 1931, the rules "nowhere lay down that past or present overseas residence is an essential qualification for membership." Between 1944 and the 1951 year of crisis, 817 members were elected, an insufficient turn-over against a greater number of deaths and resignations. Of those, 439 had lived in India, 79 in other parts of the East and 65 had other eastern connections. The other 234, just over 28 per cent, had no Oriental associations before joining the club. Of the 120 elected in 1967, slightly over 33 per cent were entirely men of the west. In 16 years the club's influx of easterners fell from three quarters to two thirds of its recruitment.

The connection with points east of the Bosphorus was slowly becoming more tenuous. Immediately after the move suggestions were made that the Oriental Club was no longer an appropriate name, that it might even discourage potential members. Mr C F Maxwell argued for a name change at the 1961 annual general meeting, claiming that 'Oriental' confused taxi drivers and suggested "a shady dive in Soho." One member reported that, on returning from the east he had asked a cabby for the Oriental and soon found himself up two flights of stairs and through the bead curtains to be charged a fortune for a cocktail and a very short dance. He confessed that he did not make his lunch appointment until very late that evening. Maxwell mooted a new name, the Stratford Club, but the members soon turned him down, full of hope of further misunderstanding in taxis.

A more obvious change in the nature of the membership was the innovation of female associates. Women had enjoyed the club since 1951. Now, in the mid-1960s, the club was not economically viable without them and, to the horror of the remaining dinosaurs, quite inured to their presence. In Stratford House they were forbidden five rooms: the bar and the smoking room, presumably because lewdness might there be spoken; the dining room, because they had their own more exclusive dining room looking into the courtyard; the billiards room; and the downstairs gent's, although there never was a formal rule there. The billiards room welcomed women by the end of the century.

Just as crucial to the success of the club, and just as much a consequence of Stratford House, was a new youth in its membership. Mere brats in their forties were now joining so that not only did the new clubhouse seem more lively than Hanover Square but the club also now could count on some longevity from its members. The marginalisation of the dinosaurs was rapid: as more younger men joined so did more of their younger colleagues and friends.

This new infant membership was impatient of some of the older traditions. Some old practices were anachronisms ready for extinction, some were a small loss, especially to the ancients. Parsons, the head valet since 1917, was a great source to Forrest. He regretted the loss of valets, servants necessary in Edward VII's reign but in little demand in the swinging sixties. He remembered when the club had three valets and several boys in attendance, all required because, as he told Forrest,

> Why, those old members would never have thought of unpacking their own suitcases; they relied on me to do that, and to lay out their evening clothes, put studs in their shirts, see that the boys ran their baths, and practically dress some of them.

Such decadence was lost after the move to Stratford House, although the club has always had one valet to supervise clothes maintenance and ensure that members wake in the mornings. It is a luxury often expected by those returning from the east.

Other indulgences were lost. Gold sovereigns had long gone out of currency so the head waiter was no longer required to weigh them for debasement before accepting payment. Now, just a few years before decimalisation, silver coins were no longer "rubbed or polished with a leather" before being given in change. Nothing now was sold at less than six pence because nothing was worth less than sixpence when once everything had cost more than half a shilling just so that members need not carry copper.

The new influx of members after 1961 might not have been quite as jolly as their predecessors. The billiards room would hardly be used for 20 years and heavy gambling on a game would be a rarity. Cards, once the prime activity of members in the Oriental, became a minority sport limited to aficionados of bridge who rarely follow Osbaldeston's example of duelling over the fall of a suit. Even the old custom of reserving a dining table by turning over the plates was lost when over-organised modern men introduced a system of booking in advance.

New men in the 60s were stern and solemn compared to the Hanover Square survivors. In the late 30s, Alice recalled, she would open nine or 10 bottles of whisky every evening for the drawing room. By the late 60s, for a room equally full, she would open only two or three. Thirty years of social engineering by obtrusive government had raised booze taxes immorally but not to that ratio; the Oriental had become less liquid. Old eccentrics could still confound sobriety: one, after drink, would roam the club obsessively unplugging all the lights and electric sockets. Another would go home sober but insist on staying at the club when drunk on the condition that he was given a room with all black bed and decorations. A third would go to bed early but rise in the small hours, sit in his nightshirt by the drawing room hearth and return to his room only if led by the hand by Alice. All these and many others were indulged with varying degrees of patience and cheerfulness.

In the closing comments of his 1968 history Forrest wrote:

> It is possible, of course, that the next generation of members, queuing up at the self-service counter or buying their drinks from an automatic machine, will look back on 1968 with nostalgia. They may even come to regard the present membership as a delicious set of old oddities.

His prediction was half right.

AFTER A HUNDRED and fifty years in which the Oriental Club had suffered every financial misfortune from a secretary emigrating with its money to a slowly decaying membership, it emerged in 1974 to celebrate its 150th birthday as one of the only secure and safe clubs in London. Others had suffered the same ailments that had threatened the Oriental during the 'fifties: competition from hotels and homes; rising expenses; recession in various relevant parts of the economy; tax; and a shrinking recruitment base. The Oriental, however, was financially secure as a result of Bruce's, Bridgland's and Wellington's economic foresight. Members were never smug, of course, but they knew that they were safe from the carnage in St James's and Pall Mall.

The Company officers who had founded the Oriental in 1824 did so partly because they felt unwelcome in other clubs. One, the United Service Club, the 'Senior', might have deliberately snubbed them with a systematic campaign of blackballing. Their shades looked down with only as much *schadenfreude* as good grace would allow when, in 1976, the Senior was dissolved. Built by the Oriental's old friend Decimus Burton, it had been Wellington's second favourite club; he would have shuddered at the building's fate, to be filled by the mere tradesmen of the Institute of Directors.

The Senior was not alone during the late sixties and seventies. The St James's Club, the Guards, the Devonshire and the Junior Carlton all failed. Amalgamations were so common that some clubs emerged with more dynastic barrels to their names than a Victorian heiress. Another club which had once treated the Oriental with small respect, the East India Club, became, in 1978, the East India, Devonshire, Sports and Public Schools Club Limited. That last title was the saddest: the acknowledgement of a business run by directors rather than a fellowship served by a committee of reluctant, amateur tribunes.

Lunch companions prepare for dinner in the smoking room.

Nevertheless, clubs must be commercial to survive, though with the humble objective of their own perpetuation rather than profit. If there is any business competition between London clubs it is only in the most abstract sense. The particularly clubable join everything they can afford, most join a club that has some connection with their own interests. Rivalry is usually only sporting. Yet the Oriental could feel complacent. Other clubs failed during the 'seventies because their demand shrank as fewer people were willing to become members. This was not just a consequence of oil crises and taxation. Clubs had become slightly anachronistic. The Senior had originally been founded only for officers of field and flag rank in the service of the crown. Others were not always welcoming to those who were not part of some specific group; lawyers, sportsmen, aristocrats, or clergymen. The Oriental Club had long since shed any entry qualifications other than the friendship and respect of an existing member. As such, it respected a stylish past but shunned anachronism. Its original purpose was long gone but it survived by the affection and admiration of its members and their recruits.

Of course, the comparative modernism in the soul of the Oriental was an advantage over other clubs searching for a shrinking number of people willing to become members. The Oriental had the extra advantage provided by lots of money. Two freeholds and a healthy share portfolio had rendered the club safe. Money can buy love.

Unlike the East India Club, with all its conquests, the Oriental never became a limited company. Nor was it any sort of partnership among the members. Its legal status, as owner of great property and investments, was confusingly nebulous. Cicero, Justinian and all the authors of the Napoleonic Codes missed the answer to such a strange jurisprudential conundrum: English Common Law, however, is all about inventing answers to difficult questions. The club and its membership could be defined as owners of such vast wealth only by a conceit of Common Law, in fact the mirror image of Common Law, by the peculiarly English device that peculiar English lawyers call Equity. The Oriental Club was held in trust. The club, its possessions and merely financial identity were settled by the members on trustees who, in turn, held it for beneficiaries who were, in turn, the members. The Common Law legal ownership of the Oriental fell to trustees while the equitable ownership, the supreme possession in the eyes of Chancery, lay with the members. They entered, mostly unknowing, a category that m'learned friends call an unincorporated association. Consequently, every member, with 50 years or five minutes seniority, would have an equal share of the assets should a crisis like that of 1951 recur and the decision ever be to dissolve the club.

It would not get that bad again, but the Oriental suffered as much as any other enterprise during the raging inflation of the 1970s. In 1968 salaries and wages had cost £50,955. Ten years later they cost £123,923. Rates and insurance went from £7,192 to £18,690 over the same decade and light and heating bills rose from £5,052 to £17,116. Rent from Hanover Square and income from shares provided £13,879 in 1972. That year's general reserve still had to be debited £4,506. One of the problems was that the Hanoverian ground rent was a fixed sum unprotected from inflation. In April, 1973, an extraordinary general meeting debated the sale of the freehold and the lease on Tenterden Street so that the money could be invested elsewhere. Sentiment and an atavistic knowledge that Wellington's advice about land ownership should never be forgotten won the day. No further action was taken.

Subscriptions would have to go up. They rose for the first time in 24 years when, in January, 1975, town subscriptions rose from £29 to £50 and, a year later £75 until, in 1977, it settled on a round £100. The entrance fee also increased. It had been abolished in 1952 as part of the desperate recruitment drive of the early 1950s. After the move to Stratford House the committee thought the club sufficiently attractive to reintroduce the fee at £26. In 1971 it leapt to £55, and to £75 in 1978 without greatly discouraging membership. By the second half of the decade the general reserve showed a net surplus.

Those tolerant members and their associate women presumably recognised that the price of the club rose no faster than everything else in the seventies. Their numbers were still increasing, although the rate of recruitment slowed a little after the first increase of entrance fees. In 1972 the Oriental had 1,930 members and 870 associates. Committees decided that numbers should be contained, if not reduced, and various forms and requirements for letters about the candidate were introduced. Hubris calls for Nemesis. Just as the election rules were tightened and fees and subscriptions rose, the number of new members fell into decline. Numbers had fallen below 1,800 by 1975. It was nothing dangerous but a reminder that when the Oriental Club has ever felt safe and thought its members rich it has been punished for its complacency.

The fall in recruits was soon staunched. Oriental Club sergeants wandered the world, beat the drum and dropped shillings into the beer of unsuspecting candidates. East of Aden senior members were asked to find likely young blood and come to the aid of the election committee by doing a little research about the good prospects. By 1977 the ranks were once more swelling.

Naturally, this new membership had all the usual eastern connections. Hong Kong, rather than India, was now the most common outpost of the club's empire, and East Africans, only oriental by the strictest application of the Bosphorus test, were an increasing contingent. Just as the first recruitment campaign in 1824 had caused confusion and selected members randomly and often careless of their desire to join, the mid-1970s intake from the East did not always enjoy complete freedom of choice. Nobody was actually Shanghaied but a small number found, when they got home, that the club was an expense that they could not justify. As had been the case 150 years before, a few who happily joined in Singapore or Sri Lanka resigned in London. Most remained.

Crucially, the Oriental had now escaped its image as the shelter of genteel geriatrics. So glad was the committee, in February, 1972, that a majority of members could climb the stairs unassisted that it surveyed dates of birth. In 1978, 29 per cent of members would have achieved the almost juvenile age of just 65 years; 12.5 per cent would still be under 40. The oldest member was 98, the youngest 18. Such a profile was much younger than most other clubs could boast. It was not all that much older than the increasingly ancient national adult average. Importantly, the club could confidently hope that its members would survive long enough to enjoy years of expenditure in Stratford House.

By the end of the decade the Oriental had built on all the work of Bruce and Bridgeland. Its wealth was secure, its operations as profitable as the economy would allow and its membership growing and promising longevity. The only problem was an enormous hole under the clubhouse.

DEEP UNDER Stratford House, 101 feet and nine inches beneath the foundations, a great chasm was opened through the ground. London Underground started work on the Fleet Line north of Oxford Street in 1971. On the 20th of October the committee noted the proposed use of Debenham's car park just across Marylebone Lane to the east of the club, as the works site for the excavations. Two possible problems arose from the tunnel: the works site might easily restrict access to the courtyard; the subterranean, Orphean disturbances might harm the fabric of Stratford House, sitting as it did on Aldborough's slim foundations.

The works site was a noisy neighbour for ten years but its only real impact was to provide an interesting view from the eastern bedroom windows. When the site was cleared in the early 1980's it left a derelict hole and then, eventually, a multi-story carpark with an elegant, tessellated design and a dark shadow cast on the club in the mornings, when shadow is most welcome. Other works at the south end of Stratford Place were eventually cleared away by London Transport, only to be replaced by perpetual builders.

Actual digging and the trains that must follow were more frightening prospects. A sub-committee created to monitor the situation remembered Lord Derby's complaints that the old electric trains of the Central Line "brought down" parts of Stratford House in 1900. By the time trains started running in 1977, now as the Jubilee Line, very little damage had been done. Some cracks had appeared in the office and the library ante-room. London Transport compensated with £1,620 and offers of further money for any further harm. A few members complained of faint vibrations in the silent hours but, in the presence of Guthrie's ghost, the trains are not proved guilty.

Deeds are more powerful than words and the words in the deeds of Stratford House gave the owners of the property not only the traditional rights over the soil unto the centre of the Earth but also over the soil under Stratford Place unto Oxford Street. For the freedom to burrow under the clubhouse the club generously asked the Greater London Council for only £1,000. The council paid a mean £520. Rights to the sub-soil of Stratford Place, to which the club was entitled by Common Law and natural justice, were simply stolen by the statutory theft of a private act of Parliament.

When the Jubilee Line was opened it was generally welcomed by members. They had always appreciated the fast access to the City provided by the Central Line, whatever Derby's horror stories, and the new route, also stopping at the club's private Bond Street Station, opened up north-west London and a quick trip to Charing Cross and the south-east of England. Such access was all the more welcome: what London Transport gave underground was taken on the surface. Oxford Street was dedicated to buses and taxis in 1972. Planners claimed that the measure was a temporary experiment. The temporary experiment involved the widening of pavements and the planting of trees. The planners were deceivers but the improvement in the flow of mechanised traffic on Oxford Street was undeniable. Pedestrian traffic became almost intolerable during shopping hours: on a hot day the Cairo souk was more tranquil. Smaller streets parallel to Oxford Street took up the burden of private cars, polluting Marylebone but not particularly impairing access to the club's courtyard car park off Marylebone Lane. The changes probably benefited most members: the courtyard could accommodate little more than a dozen cars; Oxford Street was open to private vehicles in the evenings; and taxis and later minicabs had always been the favourite mode of transport from, if not to the club. All would have been perfect if only the Tube could have been cleaned and made to run all night. Even the closure of Bond Street Station around midnight could only contribute to the club's bedroom occupancy.

The Oriental's environs suffered much indignity for the sake of modern transport.

The clubhouse itself had been suffering even longer from traffic pollution. Clouded by carbon smoke, Aldborough's facade was a dark and smoky visage. Cleaning operations started in late 1972, costing £1,758.30 and another £250 for minor repairs. Aldborough's economical sense of building was revealed: the stonework was found to be only a few inches thick, pegged to a brick wall by concealed iron spikes.

Ever since the first bedrooms were opened in Hanover Square the demand for accommodation had increased. Four more were built on the flat roof of Derby's extension to the east of the courtyard. A plumbing system was disturbed by falling masonry during construction. The seriousness of the fault was not noticed until, weakened by damp plaster, a ceiling painting escaped its seals and floated gracefully down upon the diners below, spinning slightly in its descent before gently draping a member bent intently over his mulligatawny. Repairs were expensively, expertly and expeditiously effected.

AS THE seventies progressed the successive committees walked a cautious line between accepting more modern standards and maintaining a rigid adherence to the club rules as they interpreted them. In a decision of transient significance but sartorial catastrophe, on the 19th of January, 1972:

> The committee considered the wording of by-law F7 - dress - and decided to make no amendments thereto. It was agreed jackets must always be worn in the club, but roll neck sweaters could be allowed if discreet in pattern.

Yet when some sailors wanted to bring Queen Elizabeth (the monarch, not the boat) to the club, in September, 1974, the committee found the conventions unchanging:

> ...the Association of Royal Naval Officers, through a member, had asked if the association could hold a reception here at which it was hoped Her Majesty would be present. The sub-committee had replied that by tradition the first floor public rooms were only available for a private party on a Friday evening and Saturday, and it was not felt possible to part from this tradition.

Nor was hospitality offered to ladies who had rejected monarchy, as recorded in December, 1973:

> The committee considered a letter from Mrs L Hindley [an associate] seeking permission to conduct a party of American ladies round the club. The committee decided not to grant permission.

Times were clearly changing and some people had no respect for venerable institutions. In September, 1974, the committee reacted with indignant restraint to a short article published in a recent number of *Private Eye:*

A new low in London Clubland was registered the other day by gifted magazine writer Anthony Haden-Guest not only being refused membership of the Oriental Club in Stratford Place (the least exclusive club in the world) but being actually frog-marched from the premises when he attempted to effect an entry.

The only club in London where he is welcome is the Colony Room where owner Muriel Belcher was heard to mutter, as she readmitted him after some years to membership: "Oh no, not that (expletive beginning with c deleted) again."

Haden-Guest who is now claiming to be in direct line to the title of Lord Haden-Guest of Salling (no relation according to Burke's peerage) was *last weekend* declared a prohibited immigrant by the Oxfordshire Constabulary after a week spent in Burford where he left a trail of unpaid bill and broken furniture which in their impact far exceeded the Windsor pop festival.

Unamused, the secretary recorded a minute of which he cannot have known the accuracy:

The committee considered an article in Private Eye of the 6th September in which the club is mentioned. After discussion it was agreed to take no action though the article is 100% inaccurate.

One hundred per cent? Might he have provided an alibi for the Burford caper?

The Oriental had clearly been wise to reject Haden-Guest. The election procedure was slowly perfected. Gradually it was realised that a proposer and a seconder should both write to an election committee with fairly full details about the candidate. Occasionally frauds were committed, often discovered when a seconder denied knowledge of his protege. Two or three times a year candidates were invited to meet the committee for further scrutiny. By the early 1980s the scrutiny was devolved onto a further four sponsors, whose recommendations must join those of the proposer and seconder. If sufficient members of the committee liked the candidate, the sponsors could be dispensed with. Those putting a friend up for the club were expected to have three or five years membership of their own. Eventually an alloy of the sponsor form and a polite drink with (and provided by) a number of committee members came to satisfy the needs of a club dependent on new members who would not steal the silver and old members who wished their friends to be entitled to buy them a drink.

Severe deception and one or two honest mistakes tested the various prototype selection systems. One member seconded Mr Godber, an acquaintance in Hong Kong. On the 12th of June, 1973, he felt obliged to write to the committee:

Regretfully, I have to inform you that there has been quite a corruption scandal in Hong Kong and it appears that Mr Godber has been under investigation for some time. News broke last night that he was going to be charged with a criminal offence but he had, in the meantime, managed to get out of the colony with his present whereabouts unknown. An arrest warrant has been issued and Interpol has been advised. As you can imagine, this development gave quite a shock to the community since Mr Godber was one

of the most senior police officers, with over 20 years service in Hong Kong....
in the circumstances, I do not consider him a suitable member of the club and
I wish to withdraw my signature as a seconder.

Fairly or not, the Royal Hong Kong Police were known as a uniformed triad for
many years. During the days when the committee sought to meet every candidate
proposers could be over-sensitive about their own judgement. One was offended that
his proposal required further investigation. Writing from Nairobi in December, 1973,
he fumed:

I refer to your letter... which infers [he meant implies, he did all the
inferring] that your committee does not consider me a competent person to
select suitable overseas members... I shall myself be in England in the spring
and summer but shall probably prefer to use the East India and Sports Club
where I have been a member for many years.

A few weeks later he had a greater understanding of the general rule about the
committee's interest in candidates and exclaimed:

Please thank the committee for their kind remarks. I am truly attached to
the club and hope to use it for another 20 years! I hope the noise is a little less
by now! I shall be in England in the spring and look forward to seeing you. I
hope things are not too awful for you all.

Such kindly sentiments were not universal. Various methods of investigating
candidates could exclude the real villains. Guests, however, were beyond
legislation. Since the whole purpose of the club was hospitality there was little any
committee could do to discourage members from entertaining. Guests' behaviour,
it was felt, was entirely the responsibility of their host. Misdemeanours were rare.
When trouble did occur the committee's wrath was terrible. Mr C A Day was unwise
in his choice of companions in November, 1979. Another member complained. The
incident was minuted in detail:

The nub of the complaint was the guests had remained in the bar when Mr
Day left the clubhouse and that the guests were continually using extremely
foul language... It was agreed that the following [committee] members should
meet Mr Day in the committee room viz. Sir Cyril Pitts... acting as chairman
for the evening.

Eventually, Day faced the inquisition, full of apologies, and threw himself upon
the mercy of the committee...

Sir Cyril observed that this was the first occasion in the recollection of any
of the gentlemen present that a member had been asked to appear before

representatives of the general committee. Sir Cyril stressed that the committee guarded very jealously the good reputation of the club which was highly regarded by the membership and added that the committee did not propose to tolerate any fall in standards... Mr Day tendered an unequivocal apology to the committee and undertook never to invite the same two guests to the club again. It transpired that one guest was his nephew and the other a friend of his nephew. Mr Day accepted responsibility for the incident and stated he would in the future never leave his guests in the clubhouse alone.

Two aspects of the case were strange, showing some officiousness by the committee. Firstly, by-law F12, which forbade members from leaving their guests alone, was usually fairly lax; absenteeism for the sake of the telephone or the bladder was expected and, if a member arrived after his guest the staff would usually make the guest's wait comfortable and provide a drink on the member. Leaving guests in the clubhouse was regarded as odd simply because it was so inhospitable: the poor castaways could not buy themselves a drink. Secondly, "extremely foul language" was one of the reasons for having an all male bar and, in this case, probably justly caused by the fact that memberless guests went thirsty. The magnificent Baillie's two old brother Company officers - "and the swearing, oh the swearing" - would never have objected to a robust use of language. Nevertheless, Day's troubles were just beginning.

In December, 1981, the committee received a letter from Mr R W Baxter, who had flown in from Canada with friends:

During our flight across the Atlantic I regaled them with the glories of the Oriental Club: the beauty of the building, the comfort, the service and the general air of splendour. All this continues to be true. However... we were all astonished to see and hear a very drunken young man sitting in the corner of the room near the door, yelling and whistling, arguing and swearing. This went on for over an hour, during which... the following words were heard loud and clear [Baxter gives comprehensive details of repetition and the precise context as to the noun, the verb, the participle and the gerund]. Now, Sir, I submit that language of this nature, uttered loudly in the presence of ladies, would be enough to have a man ejected even from the Pig and Whistle in Hackney High Street. On several occasions my companions restrained me from going over to the offender and creating a scene of my own. I learned later that (thank goodness) the young drunk was not a member but had been brought in by - according to the stewards - a Mr Day. I remember seeing a man of mature years talking to the lout when I entered but he left quite soon, leaving the young drunk to his own resources, which included being very insolent to your loyal staff.

The evidence was not ambiguous, the crime heinous, justice summary and swift. This second offence was more serious, no mere linguistic heritage but inconsideration for other members' enjoyment of the club and, worse, abuse of the staff. Poor Mr Day, whose own behaviour might have been modest as a nun's, was summoned back to the tribunal, his fate already sealed but a defence allowed for the sake of natural justice. Proceedings were reported to the committee in February, 1982:

(ii.) Mr Day was reminded of a previous misdemeanour and was invited to add further comments or observations... The chairman recalled that Mr Day had been informed... that his resignation, if tendered, would be accepted. Since that meeting nothing had been heard from Mr Day and in consequence... he had been invited to meet the general committee of management to make any observation he wished.

(iii.) Mr Day apologised for the behaviour of his guest and stated that he thought it was unreasonable for the committee to be considering his expulsion on account of the behaviour of a guest... Mr Day stated he had been associated with the club for 20 years, 15 as a member... He was extremely fond of the club and asked the committee to consider imposing a suspension from membership for a period rather than expulsion.

(iv.) The chairman stated the committee would take into account Mr Day's observations and the result of their deliberations would be communicated in writing to him. Mr Day then left the committee room.

(v.) After a short discussion the committee agreed unanimously to expel Mr Day from membership.

And may God have mercy on his soul. Justice was not tempered with mercy at the Oriental Club. It seems a little harsh that a man should be penalised for the actions of another but Day had broken a golden rule; he had allowed the ruin of another member's evening.

This one saga proves how determined the committees of the late 1970s and early 1980s were to preserve, at least, a friendly atmosphere in the club. They could be just as tough in the face of other, very individual, problems with members. Perhaps the most painful was the problem presented by one of the club's most loyal, respected and well-liked members. In 1976 Mr W F Byrnes had defied mortality for 93 years but, unlike the immortal Trojan princess, Apollo had not granted him eternal youth. In August, he had demanded a room in the club during the summer closure. When refused he instructed solicitors to write in complaint. He also made accusations to the chairman that on previous stays at the club items had been stolen from his room. The chairman had taken several calls from Byrnes over the holidays:

He had found him somewhat confused and it was impossible to ascertain the knub [sic] of his complaints. The chairman added that in the past and contrary to by-law E2(a) [which forbade staying at the club for more than seven nights], Mr Byrnes had been allowed to stay continuously for several months in the club, and of late had become very forgetful and difficult. The chairman said he had some sympathy with Mr Byrnes who appeared to have no surviving relations, but felt he had arrived at a time of life when he needed special and experienced help which could not be provided by the club's staff. Other members of the committee who were acquainted with Mr Byrnes said they knew he was upsetting some of the staff.

The secretary wrote to Byrnes that the rule against prolonged residence would now be enforced. After a search it was discovered, inevitably, that nothing had been stolen. The minutes continue to emphasise the committee's sympathy for Byrnes, that he was a valued and welcome member, but that he could not stay for more than a week, nor ever in August. Just as drunk young men would not be tolerated, grumpy old men could not be indulged.

The unfortunate Mr Day had been told that the committee "regarded very jealously the good reputation of the club." Occasionally, candidates for membership threatened that reputation. With no risk of wild drunkenness or offensive behaviour, the committee viewed some as a danger to the stability of the club. Conservatism still reigned at the Oriental, though such rejections were usually gentle, relations with the disappointed proposer cordial. A candidate had been interviewed by the chairman in December, 1979:

> ...a general impression had been created that [the candidate] wished to join the club mainly to use the library and the dining room for entertaining business guests and possibly to try to change slightly the club's traditions and mode of behaviour. If this indeed was the case the chairman expressed the opinion that it would not be long before the committee and [the candidate] did not see eye to eye... The chairman added that the committee had nothing personal against [the candidate].

Membership numbers had never been a serious problem for the Oriental Club since it had come to Stratford House. Twenty years later, however, without needing the numbers, it welcomed a vast new influx. For the sake of fellow feeling, rather than survival, the story of the Alfred Club was to be repeated.

WHEN THE Alfred Club had collapsed 130 years before, the Oriental had been saved from a similar fate by taking on its members. Now, in 1981, another smallish club with a cheerfully idiosyncratic reputation was in dire trouble. This time the Oriental really was benevolent; no hidden agenda lay under the kindness offered to the members of this sinking institution. The Bath Club was going down the plughole.

The Bath Club had been founded in 1894 when two members of the Carlton, Lord Desborough and Sir John Henniker-Heaton, regretted that London offered no swimming pools other than the grim pits in which they might have to share the water with all-comers. They bought the Marquis of Abergavenny's house in Dover Street, built a swimming pool in the ball room and added Turkish baths and squash courts. The pool had a distinguished future: Queen Elisabeth II and her sister learned to doggy paddle there and the Oxford and Cambridge swimming match was held there for many years. Edward VIII and George VI were coached in squash on the Bath's courts. In 1926 it enjoyed a pleasing notoriety: Captain Peter Wright had written to Gladstone's family quoting Lord Milner's opinion that the Grand Old Man "was ruled by his seraglio." These scandalous, but largely accurate words were written on Bath Club paper so the club expelled him. He sued for wrongful expulsion and lost his case only after a long and amusing trial.

P G Wodehouse once said that if his creation, the Drones Club, was based on any real institution, it was the Bath because, at the time, and disregarding the RAC as usual, they both had pools. His description in *Uncle Fred Flits By* was probably accurate:

> In order that they might enjoy their after-luncheon coffee in peace, the Crumpet had taken the guest whom he was entertaining at the Drones Club to the smaller and less frequented of the two smoking rooms. In the other, he explained, though the conversation always touched an exceptionally high level of brilliance, there was apt to be a good deal of sugar thrown about.

In 1941 the Dover Street clubhouse was accidentally burned down. The Bath moved briefly to the Lansdowne, where members could still swim, before going on to share premises with the Conservative Club in St James's Street. Eventually they merged, being christened the Lava-Tory Club. Officially still the Bath Club, it moved in 1959 to a building in Brook Street which had once housed American servicemen. There, it provided a room for the old Flyfishers Club. The Tories and the anglers, both subsumed with the bathers, had now no sporting facilities. Deprived of its *raison D'être*, the Bath faced a slow but irreversible decline throughout the 1970s.

The minutes of the Oriental committee in May, 1981, record the degree of support then offered by one club to another:

> The committee learned with regret that it was probable that the Bath Club would close on the 30th June. It was noted that the Bath Club members had been offered hospitality to the end of the year by the Naval and Military Club but it was felt that some members might prefer to join a club situated close to the Bath Club... It was agreed that the entrance fee would be waived for any Bath Club member applying to join here. The chairman stated he would write to the chairman of the Bath Club informing him of this decision.

Two months later the Flyfishers were denied such an escape. Thirty bathers had already joined the Oriental. Within the year, when the offer was closed, 157 members of the closed Bath Club had joined the Oriental. Almost 10 per cent of the membership was now from a source outside the usual Oriental recruiting ground. Just as the Alfreds had once enriched the club's culture, now, once more, the Oriental was strengthened by a new strain in its pedigree, although sugar throwing never really caught on.

The Oriental was not so welcoming to other clubs. Throughout the 1970s successive committees had found various reasons not to open reciprocal arrangements with overseas clubs. The Tanglin, the Calcutta, the Hong Kong and the Muthaiga, among many others, including several in North America as well as the Orient, suggested some sort of mutual agreement. Always, they were turned down. Two reasons were invariably given. Either a reciprocal arrangement would discourage potential members from joining the Oriental because they would have no need to if they had the club's facilities by their membership elsewhere; or the potential partner could not offer Oriental members the same quality of service that the Oriental would offer a partner's members. It was a catch-22: if the Oriental committee felt another club was good enough then it was a rival, if its facilities did not rival those of the Oriental then it would be an uneven reciprocation. By this circular logic, the Oriental could never have reciprocal arrangements with an overseas club.

During the 1980s, Oriental committees relented. They acknowledged that, in the age of international business when no city was more than 24 hours from London, the club's members could expect to enjoy the delights of its fellow clubs across the globe. Consequently, by 1993, members of the Oriental looked forward to a welcome in 14 other clubs in America and Africa, the Pacific Rim and even Scotland. Bizarrely, the great old clubs of India and the Far East, most of whom had enquired about reciprocation, were still not added to the list: they were still seen as competition, perhaps, and members in Bombay or Kualu Lumpur were expected to come back to Stratford Place for a drink.

The club still found women troublesome. On the 9th of May, 1979, for the first time in a long history during which its first and only president had often lived in 10, Downing Street, the prime minister was not eligible for full membership of the Oriental. By the time she left office in 1990 almost as many women had done business, built careers and made fortunes in the Orient as men. Female tai pans and presidents had wielded power, thousands more had served administrations or corporations in the Orient. When the club had opened in 1824 John Malcolm's definition of its membership had been:

> That all persons who have resided or travelled or whose official situation connects them with that quarter of the globe, be considered eligible to become members.

Eastern achievement had been his criterion but now that women were achieving in the East the founder's words were ignored by various committees. Associate members were as welcome, as necessary as ever, but they would still be disenfranchised. In September, 1982, the secretary received one of many similar letters:

> Dear Sir,
>
> I wrote to you some time ago, and I wondered if you have had any change in policy, and now admit women in their own right to your club.
>
> Yours truly, Elspith Creek.

At the following meeting the membership sub-committee simply recorded "nothing to report." Even the associate ladies were kept in their place. After a "social evening" in 1976 the convenor of the house sub-committee...

> reported that... critical observations had been heard that ladies had been allowed to use the bar... This raised the question of how much interference should be permitted on such evenings to the usual facilities provided by the club. With the exception of the bi-annual cocktail parties it was felt the bar should not be opened to ladies and any interference with the usual facilities should be kept to a minimum.

Fifteen years later, in June, 1991, it was minuted that:

> Consideration might be given to ladies being admitted into the main dining room at luncheon... The committee did not favour this suggestion... That a menu more suitable for ladies was to be introduced in the garden room.

At 167 years of age the Oriental Club still had problems with women.

THE ONE woman regarded with undiluted respect, with something approaching awe, by all members was Alice. By 1970 most members had not been born when she started work in the club. She had become materfamilias and patron saint, slightly frightening to those junior members who had less than a good 30 years experience, equally disciplinarian and tremendously kind to all those she regarded as needing looking after. She was already a mother figure in the 1950s, when that genial drunken sleep walker had refused to go to bed unless she tucked him in. Older than the century, in the club's service since 1916, she had become an icon of the Oriental.

In April, 1973, the first business before the committee was to record that Alice ("Miss E. Moore") was hospitalised with suspected gall stones. The committee sent her their wishes for a swift return to health. She was soon back and, after a mere 57 years at the club, the concept of retirement was gently explored. It was out of the question, very emphatically; what would her gentlemen do? It had been a silly suggestion anyway. She would have been missed too sorely to lose.

Five years later Alice became a national institution. A little natural showmanship was revealed as the BBC made a documentary, *Alice at the Oriental*, broadcast in October, 1978. The committee was delighted with her fame but would give those media types no leeway:

> It was agreed to charge the BBC a nominal fee of £50 for the facilities provided.

A month after the broadcast most members simply enjoyed seeing on their screens the mutual affection and respect between the old lady and her gentlemen. Nevertheless, there are always critics. In November the committee had one letter

> ...protesting at the content of the BBC film *Alice at the Oriental*, and suggesting the club should have vetted the material before it was screened. The secretary was instructed to inform [the complainer] that the BBC did not permit any vetting of its programmes.

In February, 1979, Alice finally realised that, at 81, the club could survive without her. The decision was forced on her by decrepitude, and the club would never continue in the same way. In February the committee noted that;

The acting chairman stated that one hour ago a letter had been received from Miss E. Moore (Alice) stating that owing to ill health she wished to retire. The committee were very sorry to learn this news and recalled with the greatest pleasure the very efficient service Alice had rendered to the club since August, 1916... In view of her current state of health the secretary was instructed to write to Alice's nephew and enquire what arrangements the family were making for her well-being.

She died in hospital in September, 1980. It was noted by the committee that...

a member of staff on duty at that time sent two wreaths - one from the members and the other from the staff - to her funeral... The club solicitor was asked to prove her will.

A pension was paid into her estate, as well as her wages for the time she was in hospital because it had transpired that her first retirement had been merely temporary: she had just turned back up for work one day and nobody would contradict her. Other funds were paid into the estate. Mysteriously, she had hoarded a little fortune in cash. In her cupboards and "small room" was found £1,210 in notes and coins. When the club solicitor and the secretary opened an envelope she had deposited in the club's strong box they found a further wad of £3,300 in cash. Her intentions for the money, if any, were unknown.

Alice was the most famous and longest serving member of staff. Others, though had run her record close. Sixty-four years was a tough record to break but others, in the old tradition of the Oriental, had dedicated a lifetime's work.

In January, 1974, the committee had learned, "with regret," of the retirement of Miss Wiseman, a linen room maid who had been at the Oriental for 25 years. As Miss Wiseman left, Miss Sylvina Martinez was employed as a waitress. Twenty years later she too was thanked by the committee, more tangibly now, with a £7,500 gratuity. Mr J Bomba, the club's valet, retired after 23 years in 1990. Twenty or 25 years were not much compared to Alice's 64 years, but they were still impressive epochs, typical of the longevity of the Oriental's staff.

Other members of staff have since competed with Alice for long tolerance of the members. Ramm, who seems never to have had initials nor first name, took up office as barman in 1935. During his tenure he could reportedly remember the name and preferred drink of any member who walked into the bar even if they had not seen each other for a decade. After being knocked off his bicycle in 1975 he took some time off with a broken collar bone, during which period the secretary ran the bar. Ramm was not pleased with the small changes in its layout. After 48 years, in February, 1983, he agreed that, until his retirement the next year, an assistant would be useful. Ramm drove a hard bargain:

...it was agreed to offer Ramm one more year's service on the condition that he would accept an assistant... Ramm declined to work under these conditions, but suggested he should be the assistant to a newly appointed barman... From the 5th April Ramm will work part time mornings only.

One woman came close to Alice's record. In 1988 Kathleen King, guardian of the dining room cash desk and keeper of the club's morals, retired after 48 years at the Oriental, and continued part-time for another decade.

Some of her colleagues and successors have chalked up decades. Since most members joined on the mortal side of 40 few of them can ever have hoped to be associated with the club for so many decades. And since the club has always been a construction of its human character much more than the creation of mere buildings and booze, it must be that it is those who have served and welcomed its members, and the children and even grand-children of its members, who have given the Oriental its characteristic and continuous hospitality. Lord Derby's study faced the road so that he could collect the post through the window. Since 1962 it has been the club's bar, so that those arriving by tube or taxi are observed and most have had their usual drink poured before they have asked for it. Upstairs, evening caprice and morning regrets have been equally indulged in obscure malts or precisely refined Bloody Marys and aspirin. In the dining room, dishes have been as classic or eccentric as members have wished. In the bedrooms, the dawn's slumbering wounded have often been treated with saintly patience before the linen has been reclaimed. At the front desk, solutions have been found to members' problems during the day, endless discussions of their philosophy patiently heard during the night. When the Oriental is 250 years old the club's members might think of Alice, Ramm and Kathleen as only the founders of a lasting tradition of continuous, familiar welcome.

Of course, there were rogues, though never among long-term staff. Around Christmas, 1976, the secretary reported;

> ...a dispense barman's stock float had been found to be £130 short and was taken to court. He pleaded guilty and was fined £50 and ordered to make restitution to the club.

A month later the convenor of the house sub-committee had to tell his colleagues that the secretary's room had been burgled of an antique clock, a very fancy Zeiss camera and "a quantity of new half pennies": The police had been informed. The convenor stated that the secretary was of the opinion that the burglary was an "inside job."

By 1985 the club's best security arrangements were failing: £1,600 in cash and cheques were stolen from the house manager's office. This was no romantic safe breaker with stethoscope and dynamite. He just stole the whole safe:

> There seemed no doubt that it was an inside job, and investigations were proceeding... it was agreed to ask the club's insurance brokers to advise on the suitability of the existing safes, all of which are well over 25 years old.

Members presented their receipts for that evenings takings for comparison to the counterfoils. The culprit was bang to rights. Within a week the head waiter was dismissed for fraud, though the safe was never recovered.

Pilferors inside the club, even those who took a safe, could soon be dealt with. More sinister felons outside, even on the corner of Stratford Place, could still maim those associated with the Oriental. On the 8th of November, 1985, two members of staff, Branko Galic and Simon Mellor, were mugged actually inside the National Westminster Bank on Oxford Street opposite Bond Street tube station. They had just cashed the staff pay cheque because most members of staff then preferred to receive cash. The secretary wrote to the committee:

> The staff were attacked from behind by two assailants. Mellor was coshed on the head and had to have several stitches in the wound. Branko was also coshed or punched and had acid (type unknown) thrown in his face. He was hospitalised for two days. His eyes are, I believe, fortunately undamaged, but the inside of his mouth peeled and his throat is still sore. As I write this note he is still experiencing difficulty in swallowing... I understand the bottle containing the acid has been found and some finger prints discovered... Efforts are being made to persuade more staff to have their wages paid direct into a bank account, but I expect only limited success.

Crime prospered: the robbers got away with £4,917. The club's insurance took the loss and its staff were repaid. Nevertheless, a sad precedent had been set: the club's staff and treasure had been attacked by forces from the seething mass outside.

DURING THE nabob years of the 1980s the Oriental Club and its members enjoyed a general prosperity. The club's crucial market, the British bourgeoisie, was as healthy as it had been since the Second World War. While the traditional Oriental men had been used to dormitories and barracks and cash mess bills bashed out on battered Remmingtons with no capital k, Thatcher's children were getting comfortable with luxury hotels, computer administration and instant communication. The Oriental would not tolerate mobile telephones ("peripatetic telephonic instruments") nor even briefcases in Stratford House. Nevertheless, ignoring the chrome, smoked glass and musak, some tips could be taken from the great hotels; the Peninsular or Raffles rather than the Hiltons. A further phase of work was required on Stratford House and its infrastructure.

As always, the Oriental was conservative. It was not until September, 1988, that the committee heard the first suggestions that bedrooms have *en suite* bathrooms. The convenor of the house sub-committee showed his colleagues plans for extra bedrooms and the provision of a bath or shower room in all the old rooms. Members were to lose the potential excitement of "meeting ladies in the morning on their way to the bath." The excitement would continue for seven years. In the meantime, slightly smaller improvements were made. A romantic soul on the committee in December, 1988, stopped just short of demanding gypsy violins:

> The committee also agreed the secretary should investigate 'softening' the lighting at night and introducing candles and, possibly, tablecloths.

The secretary expressed clearly his opinion in the minutes by his use of inverted commas.

Before any major work could start to modernise Stratford House it needed to be made safe. Long and expensive work was required to turn an eighteenth century mansion into a modern club, with services enough to persuade its members that they need not endure 20 year old facilities to support the Oriental. By June, 1990, it was clear that Stratford House was dangerous. The vice-chairman...

stressed the moral obligation of the club to provide adequate fire measures.

Fifteen days after he spoke those words fire broke out in the ladies' cloakroom which, like the television room and the card room, was gutted. The committee next met two weeks later. The secretary reported that:

...three members were rescued by the Fire Brigade and that one, Professor Marshall Hall, had subsequently died in hospital, although it was not thought this was a direct consequence of the fire...the chairman and the secretary had met the Divisional Fire Officer who had opined that, had the Fire Brigade arrived 30 seconds later, a large part (if not all) of the club would have been lost along with the lives of the three rescued members... the Fire Brigade had submitted a list of recommendations and suggested that the probable cause of the fire was a cigarette.

After further talks with the London Fire and Civil Defence Authority, the Brigade, insurance experts and pyrotechnicians, it was decided that an extensive rewiring and fireproofing was needed. Just in case, the club also increased its insurance coverage against personal injury claims.

Thorn Security, the firm which fitted the alarms and smoke detectors, worked slowly. After a year they agreed that their staff should work around the clock. Consequently, on the 25th of August, 1991, their workmen were in the club all night. They managed to break into the wine stores. They became very violent.

A particularly brave waiter, Mr Fernandez, attempted to protect the club's property before realising that he needed reinforcements. At midnight, he called the secretary, who was at home that night. He arrived 45 minutes later to find that...

two fire extinguishers had been let off over three floors in the north stairwell, a number of stolen bottles of club wine had been drunk, and two club pictures had been damaged; one of them by being thrown over the stairwell. He then did an inspection of the club, with Mr Fernandez, and discovered the foreman in the secretary's bed.

Understandably, the secretary was surprised. Unimpressed by intimidation, he told the foreman to leave. He was offered violence. More Thorn men came into the room. Fernandez and the secretary were outnumbered, Fernandez was pinned down. Neither man could summon help from the police or anybody else until the secretary managed to get free and, pursued by the foreman and other Thorn belligerents, he got to the street where he found Mr Dunne, the head of maintenance, who had also been called by Fernandez. The police had to call for further officers before the Thorn men were ejected from the club.

It was like the siege of Toad Hall except that it was not at all funny. Thorn's stoats and weasels had been dishonest, destructive and dangerous. If the resistance had not been so resolute Stratford House, still vulnerable to fire, might have burned with its invaders. In the middle of the West End, the secretary, the waiter and the head of maintenance had been forced to skirmish with thieving, violent drunks to protect the Oriental Club.

Of course, the secretary believed that he did that every night in the smoking room. Presumably, the committee was increasingly appalled as the story was told:

The secretary added that Mr Fernandez had reacted with great courage in trying to protect the secretary from the violence; had shown admirable initiative in telephoning Mr Dunne to report the team's behaviour and had proved himself to have commendable presence of mind during this unusual incident. Mr Dunne had also shown great support... The chairman agreed to write to Mr Dunne and Mr Fernandez to thank them for their loyalty and assistance.

The Battle of Stratford Place was followed by some quite rigorous negotiation with Thorn. Work was eventually and often soberly completed. The club became fire-safe and substantially free of invaders.

Modernisation was now possible.

During the early 1990s work was planned and expedited. The most dramatic changes to the fabric of the club came in the middle of the decade, during the chairmanship of Berry Templeton, who died in 1998. All the bedrooms gained a bathroom or shower-room, as well as redecoration. If a member now worried about meeting a lady on the way to the bathroom he took that risk by choice not necessity. A new carpet was made for the drawing room as close as possible to an eighteenth century model, although that chamber was an eighteenth century ballroom so its carpet is particularly artful and rarely danced upon. The bar benefited from new carpets during the mid-90s, and much new furniture so that, for the first time in many years, members could appreciate the club-like tradition of leather chairs. Ceiling and wall paintings were cleaned; when dull, gilt decoration was made to shine.

All this complemented a longer campaign of modernisation. As far back as January, 1973, the committee had contemplated a letter from Mr M C Riches:

...I wonder whether the committee would consider the use of some credit cards eg Access... from my point of view I would find it so convenient that I would be prepared to consider making some contribution towards this, if it were practical... you would probably also have to do the same with Barclaycard for the benefit of our members in the other camp.

A man before his time: two decades later, on the 15th of December, 1992...

The committee agreed to introduce Visa, Access, Mastercard, Delta and Switch cards as this spread would cover all the UK banks.

Even computers were accepted as a crucial part of club management. The idea of such machines first arose in October, 1990, when the committee enjoyed a presentation on the fantastical equipment. All accounts and bookings were handled on screen within a few years.

In 1814, perhaps, John Malcolm and the Duke of Wellington walked together through occupied Paris talking of their wives and power, and, unknowingly, of the politics of an emperor bound in Elba, of governing and trade, and of their friends in India, of the maharajas they once knew. Similar conversations always continued in the Oriental Club. The club they founded endured every test before, after risking collapse, it achieved the happy combination of old hospitality and modern security. Reborn in Stratford House, it proved to be reinvigorated. By the turn of the millennium the club has achieved all that Malcolm could have hoped and everything that its modern members could desire. Founded in 1824, the Oriental thrives on the prospect of the twenty-first century.

Appendix A

Founders

THE FOLLOWING names appeared on the original prospectus of the Oriental Club in 1824. The list represents the first committee.

His Grace the Duke of Wellington, KG, President.

The Right Honourable Lord William Bentinck, GCB.

The Right Honourable Charles Williams-Wynn.

Vice-Admiral Sir Richard King, Bt, KCB.

Vice-Admiral Sir Pulteney Malcolm, KCB.

Major-General Sir John Malcolm, GCB, KLS.

General Sir Alured Clarke, GCB.

General Sir George Nugent, Bt, GCB.

Lieutenant-General Sir Thomas Hislop, GCB.

Lieutenant-General Sir Miles Nightingall, KCB.

Major-General Robert Haldane, CB, Colonel, 26th Bengal Native Infantry.

Rear Admiral Lambert.

Major-General Rumley.

Colonel Baron Tuyll.

Colonel Alston.

Colonel Baillie, MP.

Alexander Boswell Esq.

David Colvin Esq.

Major Carnac.

N B Edmonstone Esq.

John Elphinstone Esq.

Major Harding.

James Hallet Esq.

D Hemming Esq.

Major-General Sir Patrick Ross.

Sir George Staunton, Bt, MP.

Sir Charles Forbes, Bt, MP.

Sir Robert Farquhar, Bt.

Sir Christopher Cole, KCB, MP.

Major-General Malcolm Grant.

Colonel Robert Houston, CB, 6th Bengal Light Cavalry.

Colonel Hull.

A Macklew Esq.

Colonel Nugent.

C E Pigou Esq.

Colonel Ranken.

Colonel George Raban, CB.

J G Remington Esq.

Thomas Snodgrass Esq.

William Sotheby Esq.

William H Trant Esq.

Henry Saint George Tucker Esq.

J Ruddell Todd Esq.

Colonel Weguelin.

Appendix B

Chairmen and Secretaries

Chairmen

Dates show years of election.

1824-1828	Sir John Malcolm.	1847-1848	James Debis De Vitre.
1828	Admiral Sir Richard King.	1849	Alexander Guthrie.
1829	Colonel William Rankin.	1850-1852	Malcolm Lewin.
1830	Lieutenant-General Robert Bell.	1853	Lestock Robert Reid.
		1854-1855	Joseph Glen
1831	Charles Edward Pigon.	1856	George Mainwaring.
1832	Robert Maconochie.	1857	Colonel William Francis Grant.
1833	Colonel Carlo Joseph Doyle.	1858	George Fleming Franco.
1834	Colonel W S Sherwood.	1859-1860	Edward Hamilton.
1835	Admiral Sir Pulteney Malcolm.	1861	Malcolm Lewin.
1836	Colonel Carlo Joseph Doyle.	1862	Edward Hamilton.
1837	Colonel Henry Purchas.	1863	Colonel William Francis Grant.
1838	Sir George Cox.	1864	Malcolm Lewin.
1839	The Rt Hon Holt Mackenzie.	1865-1866	Francis Clerk.
1840	Field Marshal Sir George Pollock.	1867-1868	Lieutenant-General Sir George St.Patrick Lawrence.
1841-1842	Sir Herbert Compton.	1869-1870	Francis Clark.
1843	Sir Edward Colbroke, MP.	1871	Alexander Henry Ross.
1844-1845	The Rt Hon Holt Mackenzie.	1872	Sir Cecil Beadon.
1846	George William Traill	1873-1875	Alexander Henry Ross.

1876	Richard Pryce Harrison.	1910-1911	David Bagne Horn.
1877-1878	Major-General C P Rigby.	1912	William Harwood.
1879	Alexander Henry Ross.	1913-1915	David Bagne Horn.
1880	Major-General C P Rigby.	1916	George Hay Alston.
1881	Sir George W Kellner.	1917	David Bagne Horn.
1882	Lieutenant-General Sir Henry Thuillier.	1918	Claude Augustus MacDonald.
1883-1884	James Alexander Crawford.	1919	Sir Stanley Bois.
1885	C T Buckland.	1920	Frank Rawson.
1886-1888	James Alexander Crawford.	1921	Richard Arbuthnot Simson.
1889-1890	George Francis Mewburn.	1922-1923	Sir Stanley Bois.
1891-1892	James Alexander Crawford.	1924	William Henry Figg.
1893	George Francis Mewburn.	1925	Ebenezer Henry.
1894	Algernon Rutter.	1926	Claude Augustus MacDonald.
1895-1896	Colonel James H Oliver.	1927-1928	William Albert Bankier.
1897-1898	Charles Joseph Lindsay-Nicholson.	1929-1930	Thomas McMorran.
1899-1901	George Henry Maxwell Batten.	1931-1932	Sir Henry Wheeler.
1902	George P Field.	1932	James McGowan (from February to May).
1903-1904	Sir William Macphearson.	1932-1933	Sir Reginald Arthur Mant.
1905	Robert J Black.	1934	Charles Findlay.
1906	Sir William Brooke.	1935	Walter Shakespear.
1907	W H McKewan.	1936	Sir Henry Wheeler.
1908	W S Shaw.	1937	Bernard Robertson.
1909	W H McKewan.	1938-1940	Sir Henry Wheeler.
		1941	Sir Alfred A Pickford.

1942	Trevor J Matthews.	1972	R Mann.
1943	Sir D B Meek.	1973	J R Carlisle Taylor.
1944	Sir Thomas Smith.	1974	The Rt Hon the Earl of Inchcape.
1945	G B Hutching.	1975	Sir John Jardine Paterson.
1946-1947	Sir Aleander Aikman.	1976	Sir Michael Parsons.
1948-1949	Roger P Slade.	1977	P Banyard.
1950	James Forbes.	1978	J Morris Gifford.
1951	Sir Charles Innes (resigned in October).	1979	Sir John Jardine Paterson.
1951-1952	James McFarlane.	1980	Sir Cyril Pitts.
1953	J K Michie.	1981	J W Ritchie.
1954	Sir Arthur Bruce.	1982	A Keown.
1955	Clve D Smith.	1983	K Gould.
1956	Sir Arthur Morse.	1984	H Hayman.
1957	Sir Robert Hutchings.	1985-1986	K Gould.
1958-1961	Sir Arthur Bruce.	1987	M G Amberton.
1962	H C Waters.	1988	T V Carter.
1963	Sir George Mackinlay.	1989	Colonel C H Martin, TD.
1964	N D Harris.	1990	R C Tucker.
1965	D F Macmillan.	1991	D Baker.
1966-1967	G S Bozman.	1992	Sir Philip Haddon-Cave.
1968	Sir Percival Griffiths.	1993	J A R R French.
1969	H T B Morison.	1994	W C L Brown.
1970	Sir Hugh Mackay-Tallack.	1995-1996	W B Templeton.
1971	J E Waterfield.	1997-1998	W C L Brown

Secretaries

1824-1838	Mr Thomas Cornish (absconded to the United States with the club's money).		1902-1908	Mr Harry Stuart.
			1908-1922	Colonel G Bird.
1838-1851	a regime of various stewards and departmental chiefs.		1922-1926	Lieutenant-Colonel H W C Wicks.
1851-1871	Mr J H Hilton (emigrated to the United States; the club paid his fare).		1926-1930	Major G C S Black.
			1930-1934	Major R C B Williams.
1871-1873	Captain W F Dadson.		1934-1937	Sir Alfred D Pickford (honorary secretary).
1873-1875	Mr Lester (general-manager).		1937-1940	Colonel A Dallas Smith.
1875-1876	Mr William Lane (secretary-manger).		1940-1945	Mr H A Gardner.
			1945-1946	Interregnum.
1876-1882	Mr Fry.		1946-1951	Mr R C Drinkwater.
1882-1887	Major Clayton.		1951-1963	Brigadier R G W Callaghan.
1887-1893	Mr Arthur Stirling.		1963-1988	Mr R N Rapson.
1893-1902	C J Pratt Barlow.		from 1988	Major S C Doble.